SOME LEADING IDEAS OF HINDUISM

SOME LEADING IDEAS OF HINDUISM

BEING THE THIRTY-SECOND FERNLEY LECTURE

DELIVERED IN MANCHESTER, AUGUST 1902

BY

HENRY HAIGH

CHIEF REVISER OF KANARESE NEW TESTAMENT

GYAN

Published by

Gyan Publishing House
5, Ansari Road
Daryaganj, New Delhi-110002
Phone: 011-47034999, 9811692060
E-mail: books@gyanbooks.com

Distribution Network
gyanbooks.com
India, USA, Canada, UK, Australia, France

ISBN : 978-81-212-2534-2 (HB)
First Published, 1903

2nd Impression 2021

Printed at: Gyan Press, Delhi.

Some Leading Ideas of Hinduism
Author: Henry Haigh

Some Leading Ideas of Hinduism

BEING THE THIRTY-SECOND FERNLEY LECTURE

DELIVERED IN MANCHESTER, AUGUST 1902

BY

HENRY HAIGH

CHIEF REVISER OF KANARESE NEW TESTAMENT

London

CHARLES H. KELLY

2 CASTLE ST., CITY RD., AND 26, PATERNOSTER ROW, E.C.

1903

TO

MY WIFE

SHARER FOR MANY YEARS

OF ALL

MY THOUGHT AND WORK IN INDIA

WITHOUT WHOSE HELP AND STRONG ENCOURAGEMENT

THIS VOLUME

WOULD PROBABLY NOT HAVE BEEN WRITTEN

PREFACE

THE Fernley Lecture as delivered in Manchester last year was the barest outline of what is contained in the present volume. I undertook the delivery of it at that time to meet an emergency, and had to make what preparation I could while greatly pressed by other and more immediate duties. It was a condition of my undertaking the task at all then that the publication of the Lecture should follow at some later period. To the Trustees of the Fernley Board I am greatly obliged for the indulgence which has been so patiently extended to me.

The subjects treated in this volume are, some of them, difficult, and they do not lend themselves readily to popular exposition. Yet that is what I have here attempted. I have desired to help the people of England to realise to themselves, as far as may be, the religious and philosophical standpoint of many of the people of India, and I have tried to do this in language as little technical as possible. Again and again, while writing these pages, I have almost despaired; but the attempt is well worth making, and he who best succeeds will have done an important work of mediation between East and West. It is especially worth while to impress upon English Christians the idea that the work of evangelising India is one that will make demand on their best intelligence and their most patient enthusiasm. Missionary success in the West —in West Africa and the West Indies—was swift and exciting; but it is a far cry from there to India. It is a change from simplicity to complexity, from animalism and the lower forms of emotionalism to the environment of the subtlest forms of philosophy, from the crudest and most fluid social organisation to the most elaborate and the most rigid. Changed conditions require changed methods. The people of India must not be expected in an hour to shed the assumptions of a lifetime inherited from centuries, as a snake sheds its skin. Casual, rapid, emotional work can afford no hope of wide and worthy success among the Hindus. Head and heart both are required for the great enterprise in India, and the former as much as the latter. It will be a great gain when the churches of this land have made this plain to themselves, and planned their campaign suitably to the special character of their enterprise.

I do not claim any originality for this volume. I cannot trace all my obligations. The reading of many years has entered into me, and found confirmation and illustration in long intercourse among the people of India. I would here make acknowledgment of much indebtedness which I am unable more particularly to specify. I have had the great advantage of reading two recent volumes by brother missionaries in South India, and to these I have again and again been indebted. One is a small volume, only published in India, by the Rev. E. W. Thompson, M.A., on *The Teaching of Swâmi Vivêkânanda;* and the other, a larger volume, by the Rev. T. E. Slater, on *The Higher Hinduism in relation to Christianity.* These books are worth the attention of many besides missionaries. And no writer on Indian thought can afford to overlook Principal Gough's most valuable book, *The Philosophy of the Upanishads.*

For the Index at the end of this volume I am indebted to a friend who desires to be unnamed, but whose kindness must not go without grateful acknowledgment.

HENRY HAIGH.

CONTENTS

INTRODUCTORY

PART I

TRANSMIGRATION

PART II

HINDU PANTHEISM

SOME LEADING IDEAS OF HINDUISM

Introductory

It will be my business in this lecture to lead you along unaccustomed paths, and to ask you to breathe an unfamiliar air. To the Englishman whose interests are mainly religious, India generally presents itself as a land of innumerable temples, peopled by gods of strange name and forbidding feature. He pictures to himself the gathering of dark-skinned devotees at religious festivals, swarming multitudes of them, each with the symbol of his deity blazoned on his forehead, and often obtruded also on his arms and breast. He sees idol-cars and swinging hooks, priests and dancing girls, instruments and incense; he gazes on the forms, distorted and malodorous, of numerous ascetics; he hears the weird chanting of frequently arriving pilgrims, the busy clamour of multitudinous tongues, and he says to himself, "This is Hinduism." Nothing could seem more unreflecting, nothing less devout. The people appear to be the victims of a silly but cheerful superstition—a superstition which, however degrading, supplies them, in its organised form, with the most festive and picturesque days of their life.

All this, however, is but the scenic and popular side of Hinduism; that which gathers the crowd and evokes the enthusiasm, which appeals to the young, pleases the old, and binds the women in convinced adherence. But Hinduism is, of course, much more than all this. At the back of all the show and movement of temple services and religious fairs there are great controlling ideas; ideas inherited from centuries, and now transformed into the fundamental assumptions of the people's whole thought and life. This becomes evident immediately when one converses with them on the seeming extravagances and puerilities of their religious observances. Let a young missionary, for instance, standing in front of an idol temple, expostulate with the people on the dishonour done to God and the degradation brought on man, by the practice of idolatry. They will listen with patience and the most punctilious courtesy. He may point to the ugliness of the image, and they will not resent it; he may assert its helplessness, and they will not deny it; he may insist that God is one, and they will all instantly acquiesce. But when he thinks they are impressed they conclude the conversation by saying:—"You have spoken true words. God *is* one, and God is *here*, in this image; here, therefore, as custom dictates and convenience suggests, we worship Him." Then the young missionary knows that idolatry, which had seemed to him the supreme evil against which he must fling himself, is only the symbol of something subtler and more elusive far—Pantheism! Not that his village hearers understand Pantheism. They can neither expound it nor defend it; but that which Pantheism means is of the very fibre of all their thinking about God, and until that is changed the worship of idols will seem natural and inevitable. Or, again, this young missionary, visiting one of the great fairs, will stumble on an ascetic holding his arm high in air. He is told that for a dozen years that arm has been held thus, in spite of all laws of gravitation, until the whole body has become distorted and the man has lost the power to recall the devoted limb. Here, then, he sees another of the extravagances of popular Hinduism, and common humanity compels him to protest against such fearful self-torture. But what says the man himself? "I am trying to cut short the eighty-four!" That is cryptic; but when the foreigner inquires he finds himself face to face with the weird but enthralling doctrine of transmigration! Then, if he be wise, he will cease to fight merely or mainly with the phenomena of Hinduism, and begin to deal with those great ideas which produce and control them.

It is the purpose of this lecture to set forth some of these great ideas. Hinduism is not a homogeneous whole, lending itself readily to definition or description. Perhaps it is now, as Barth suggests, next to impossible to say what Hinduism really is, where it begins and where it ends.[1] It certainly includes within itself many incongruous and diverse elements, derived from widely different sources; and to an extent beyond parallel it is split up into sects, each of which has its separate *shibboleth*, its distinctive ritual, and its peculiar discipline. But there is a heritage of teaching which is common to all; and there are, besides, certain other doctrines which, if not accepted by all, have yet influenced all profoundly, and may be fairly

[1] *The Religions of India*, pp. 153, 154.

said to be characteristic of the nation. It is with some of those common doctrines, such as transmigration, and some of those other doctrines from which no Hindu really escapes, even if he does not subscribe to them, such as Vedântic Pantheism, that I shall try to deal in the following pages.

It will not, I think, be denied that there *is room and need for the Christian Church to deal with such topics.* The world is rapidly drawing closer together, and the thoughts of Asia are beginning in many ways to send over an arresting challenge to Europe and America. Mr. Meredith Townsend has very properly pointed out that, while increase of communication between the continents makes it easier for us to pour in on Asia as a flood our science and literature and religion, it also "facilitates the reflex action of Asiatic ideas on Europe."[1] If in the growing wealth and luxury of the West men are losing their hold on a personal God and chafing at a religion that imposes sharp restraints and preaches self-denial, they will be likely enough to lend an indulgent ear to those doctrines of the East, which reduce God from a Personal Will to a mere pervading essence, which permit a shifting basis of morals, and give to every man an indefinitely long probation, with assured salvation at the end. Perhaps the danger may not be exigent, but few who can judge will deny that it is real.

There is, however, a fact of far more urgent importance. The Christian propaganda in India is steadily extending, and it is essential that the Church in the West should make clear to itself the unique difficulty of the enterprise

[1] *Asia and Europe*, p. 137.

to which it stands committed, and in the light of that new knowledge should review its methods and train itself to truer appreciations and more reasonable expectations. That Christianity has won substantial success in India is beyond a doubt, and every new census makes the fact more impressive. It would be strange if it were otherwise, for many outside forces are, incidentally and unintentionally, co-operating with the distinctively Christian forces which are at work there. But the great decisive conflict between Hinduism and Christianity has still to take place; and while in that conflict spiritual experience and organised human kindness will play an essential and incalculably important part, the hardest and longest and most critical fight will be one of fundamental ideas. It is imperative, therefore, that the Christian Church should, for itself, learn as much as may be of the strength and subtlety of the systems it must needs encounter. It will then seek, as never before, to ensure that those to whom it commits the responsibilities of actual warfare shall have the fullest equipment, not only of missionary zeal, but of sympathetic knowledge. For it must never be forgotten that Hinduism is a really great system. Not at Rome, nor yet at Ephesus, nor even in Athens, did the Apostle Paul ever encounter such a system as meets us in India. The systems represented by those names were all born after Hinduism, and they have now been so long dead that any reference to them to-day is merely a reference to very ancient history. But Hinduism lives on. Age has not decayed it, rivals have not destroyed it. It properly demands, therefore, from any who dream of supplanting it, the respect of thoughtful attention. It is a pleasure to acknowledge that Indian missionaries, of all names, are giving such attention to it increasingly. They confess to themselves that really impressive criticism—such criticism as will move a strong man or a great nation—can only come from the sympathies, appreciations, and disappointments of an esoteric view. They realise, I think, better than ever before, that without this no body of men, however zealous and determined they may otherwise be, can hope to rouse Hinduism or any other system to its utmost resistance and thus compass its final defeat.

Of all teaching comprehended within the system of Hinduism, the most important and the most difficult is the Vedânta philosophy. It is not among the Hindus by any means a universally accepted philosophy, but it is by far the most pervasively influential, and even those who would not formally subscribe to it are nevertheless largely permeated by it. It is in that philosophy that Christianity will find its latest, subtlest, most alert and most tenacious antagonist in India; and it is for that reason that I have tried to fix attention upon it in these pages. It has not been possible for me to treat it in any sense exhaustively; I shall be thankful if, to some extent, I have dealt with it suggestively. In all that has been written, I have had in mind not merely the Christian churches of this land, but the people in India, with many of whom I was privileged for a period of twenty-five years to hold intimate and affectionate intercourse. Even when I have not referred to it, I have tried always to see their point of view, to appeciate their reasons, and to do justice to their aims. I trust nothing has been set down which misrepresents their positions, as I am sure that no criticism has escaped me which is not born of sympathy and desire for truth. India will yet have a great influence on Christianity. The people of that land, released from the throttling grip of Vedântism, will elucidate and emphasise some aspects of Christ's teaching which have not yet made their due appeal to the people of the West; so that we, without them, cannot be made perfect. Everything that hastens their emancipation and ingathering has value, and I pray that this lecture may help to that end.

PART I

Transmigration

"And His disciples asked Him, saying, Rabbi, who did sin, this man, or his parents, that he should be born blind?"—JOHN ix. 2.

"I the Lord search the heart, I try the reins, even to give every man according to his ways, according to the fruit of his doings."—JER. xvii. 10 (R. V.).

"Who plants mangoes, mangoes shall he eat;
Who plants thorn-bushes, thorns shall wound his feet."—
INDIAN PROVERB.

"Man is only what he becomes—profound truth; but he becomes only what he is—truth still more profound."—AMIEL'S JOURNAL, p. 40.

"We shape *ourselves* the joy or fear
Of which the coming life is made,
And fill our future atmosphere
With sunshine or with shade.

The tissues of the life to be
We weave with *colours all our own*,
And in the field of destiny
We reap *as we have sown*.

Still shall the soul around it call
The shadows which it gathered here,
And, painted on the eternal wall,
The past shall reappear."—WHITTIER.

"My son, the world is dark with griefs and graves,
So dark that men cry out against the heavens."—
TENNYSON.

"The clouds which rise with thunder slake
Our thirsty souls with rain;
The blow most dreaded falls to break
From off our limbs a chain."

"In whom we have our redemption, the forgiveness of our sins."—
COL. i. 14.

"Can it be true, the grace He is declaring?
Oh, let us trust Him, for His words are fair!
Man, what is this, and why art thou despairing?
God shall forgive thee all but thy despair."—
F. W. H. MYERS, "ST. PAUL."

TRANSMIGRATION

Be not deceived; God is not mocked; for whatsoever a man soweth, that shall he also reap.—GAL. vi. 7.

Our deeds still travel with us from afar,
And what we have been makes us what we are.

Thou wast a God that forgavest them, though Thou tookest vengeance of their doings.—PSALM xcix. 8.

WE begin with an idea which is universal among the Hindus, but which also stretches far beyond them. Probably no theory has ever had a longer life or wider acceptance than the theory of transmigration. How it began or where nobody quite knows, but it has been discovered in varying forms among people as widely sundered in distance as the North American Indians and the negroes of the Gold Coast; as widely sundered in civilisation as the ancient Egyptians and the aborigines of Australia; as widely sundered in capacity as the old philosophers of Greece and the Dayaks of Borneo; and as widely sundered in creed as the Kabbalistic Jews and the Manichæans. A theory which has reckoned among its adherents, though in different senses and with unequal emphasis, such men as Pythagoras and Empedocles, Plato, Plotinus, and Origen, and which in more modern times has greatly attracted (to name no other) the strong mind of Lessing,[1] has had a remarkable history.

But the doctrine of transmigration has found its most congenial home in Asia, and Asia owes it to India. How it developed there is matter of much conjecture. It seems quite certain that the early Âryan settlers in India held no such belief. In the Rig Veda, a collection of hymns representing the best literary activity of the Âryans for some hundreds of years[2] after their settlement, there is not a trace of it.[3] Perhaps these emigrants found the doctrine in crude suggestion among the aborigines, but even so they were slow to adopt it and slower still to elaborate it. For it is not until we reach the Upanishad period of Indian literature, some six centuries before Christ, that we find the doctrine in its complete development. By that time, however, it was firmly established, and it has ever since held unquestioned sway. "There is perhaps no more remarkable fact in the history of the human mind than that this strange doctrine, never philosophically demonstrated, should have been regarded as self-evident for 2500 years to every philosophical school or religious sect in India, excepting only Materialists."[4] It was somewhere between the sixth and fourth centuries B.C. that Buddha

[1] "Why should not every individual man have existed more than once upon this world? Is this hypothesis so laughable merely because it is the oldest? . . . Why should I not come back as often as I am capable of acquiring fresh knowledge, fresh expertness?"—*The Education of the Human Race*, 94, 95, 98. Translated by F. W. Robertson.

[2] *Sanskrit Literature*, by A. A. Macdonell, p. 45.

[3] Perhaps there is one, but that is doubtful, and in any case so slight as to be of small consideration. "Its earliest form is found in the *S'atapatha Brâhmaṇa*, where the notion of being born again after death and dying repeatedly is coupled with that of retribution."—Macdonell, p. 223.

[4] *Sanskrit Literature*, p. 387.

arose. Whatever else of his ancestral creed he repudiated, he adopted the theory of transmigration whole-heartedly, simply modifying it in such detail as the rest of his system necessitated. Through him it passed forth out of India and found an abiding home in Thibet and Tartary, in Central Asia and Southern Siberia, in Ceylon, Burmah and Siam, in China, and even in Japan. It is thus clear that transmigration is no worn-out speculation, a mere curiosity of ancient belief. It is the unhesitating and fundamental assumption of more than half the human race to-day. To tell any of these people that they never lived before, and that after death they will perhaps never appear on earth again, would be to discredit one's self in their eyes as a simpleton, or to degrade one's self as an infidel. Though the stronghold of the doctrine is in the East, it is beginning to invade the West also. Alike in Germany, England, and the United States, men and women are discussing it increasingly, and are telling themselves that it is certainly interesting and not wholly unconvincing. What, then, is this theory? What are its attractions and support? Wherein lies its weakness?

I

Whatever may have been the origin of the transmigration theory, it is undoubtedly an attempt to interpret suffering. The burden that oppresses the Hindu is not sin, but existence and its attendant miseries. Like all the rest of us, he finds himself swathed in mystery. There is the mystery of physical pain "so acute sometimes that it seems the one over-mastering reality in a world of shadows," and of mental depression "so deadly that it welcomes physical pain itself as a relief." There is the mystery of our common nature and environment. Part beetle and part butterfly, that is what we all seem to be—a gruesome compound of lofty desire and mean necessity. We have capacity, but it is foiled for want of opportunity; taste, but it is over-ridden by circumstance; ambition, but it is hindered by weakness. Then there are the inequalities of life! Some are rich, who seldom work; others are poor, though they work without ceasing. Crookedness somehow prospers, and honesty walks in rags. These things are a constant puzzle to our intelligence, a ceaseless challenge to our sense of justice. Most perplexing of all, perhaps, are the inequalities of birth! One child comes into the world blind, and must live his life in unrelieved night; another is born epileptic, and his life, as it develops, is a harassment to his friends and a growing despair to himself. One begins life with a handicap of deformity, another with a heritage of disease. *Why* should these things be? We all know the weariness of this problem. In all lands and through all ages men have guessed and guessed and passed it on—the perennial riddle of history.

But to this riddle the Hindu furnishes an arresting answer. He shares the general conviction of mankind that death does not end all. Some where, some time (he believes), the life that passes from our vision here is recommissioned for service or for suffering. Moreover, he holds the conviction, holds it in its strongest form, that the life hereafter will be strictly determined by the life that we live here. Deeds are seeds, and every sowing brings its harvest, infallibly and inexorably. But if this life projects itself beyond death, and what we do now determines what we shall be then, *why may we not turn the process backward?* What if to-day and every day were determined in principle and detail by what we were before? If this life be, perchance, the fruitage of a previous life, then is the riddle solved—inequality is explained: pain must be retribution, pleasure reward, and justice is for ever vindicated!

It is an illuminating guess. If it be true, the successful man is rendered for ever indifferent to the envy of his neighbours, for has he not earned his prosperity? While the unfortunate man is no longer stung into yet acuter suffering by a rankling suspicion of injustice, but learns to submit with acquiescence to that which he assumes he must have deserved, even to the uttermost farthing of it. But apart from the comfort which this doctrine is felt to bring—the serene complacency and the soothing resignation—are there not other possibilities in it? Is it not a mighty moral engine, an incentive to virtue, a deterrent to vice? When I look at the great and prosperous, I am surely encouraged to hope that by careful conduct *I* too may enjoy the boon which has come to them. Is not the path clear, the goal certain? On the other hand, the misery around me, and not least my own, is a perpetual warning against evil.

It is thus, that on the surface and at first sight, this doctrine strikes most men. But let us contemplate it a little more closely, and set down for ourselves some of its necessary assumptions. To begin with, *it clearly demands an eternity behind us well as before.* What I suffer or enjoy now is, according to the hypothesis, the result of that which I was and did then; but that which I was then was necessitated by what I had been the birth before that, and so on indefinitely. Where would you stop? You are at once committed to an eternal series of antecedents, an endless (and beginningless) chain of cause and effect, each link of which hangs on the preceding, and the whole on —— ? Such a position, as Professor Orr has said, is "unthinkable and affords no resting-place for the reason."[1] Further, if births are eternal, *so also must the souls be* in which these ûnbeginning causes shall work out their unending effects. When, therefore, a child is born, we are not to understand that a new soul is created. What has happened is that an eternal entity—one of an innumerable company—has just taken on a fresh embodiment.

> Nay, but as when one layeth
> His worn-out robes away,
> And taking new ones, sayeth,
> "These will I wear to-day!"
> So putteth by the spirit
> Lightly its garb of flesh,
> And passeth to inherit
> A residence afresh.[2]

Once more, *the soul is not restricted in its embodiments*—that is a third assumption of the transmigration theory. This may seem less wildly incredible, perhaps, if we remember how fundamentally the Hindu conception of "soul" differs from our own. To *us* "soul" is the essential man, personality that knows itself, "the 'I' of individual experience," that reasons, wills, loves, and hates; and which

[1] *Christian View of God and the World*, pp. 115, 116. Even S'ankarâchârya, in a moment of candour, ridicules the idea of cause producing and being produced by its own effect, through an eternal series, and says it would be like "an endless chain of blind men leading other blind men."—*Vedânta-Sûtras* (*S. B. E.*), II. ii. 37.

[2] *The Song Celestial*.—EDWIN ARNOLD.

finds in the human bodily organism the only instrument through which it can properly express itself. It does not occur to *us* that a self-conscious intelligence can unite itself harmoniously with any other than the human type of physique. In all lands and through all recorded times the difference between even the lowest human and the highest animal has been so fundamental and insistent, that the ultimate commingling of the two has been regarded by us as one of the fixed impossibilities, of the same class as the union of fire and water, or light and darkness. But to the Hindu this is rank nonsense, because of his conception of soul. For to him "soul" is not the Ego. *That* he grades as matter; a very subtle differentiation of it, but still matter. It is the impalpable threefold sheath of the soul, but not the soul; its psychic body [1] merely, accompanying it through all its wanderings. What, then, is the soul itself? It is simply the vital principle that runs through Nature, "which is without thought, emotion, will, self-consciousness, or indeed any other quality whatever except that of extension and life." [2] *Such* a principle may, from the absence of any definite qualities of its own, easily invest itself in any shape required, even as water suits itself to any vessel that is at hand to contain it. To the Hindu the human is not a separate and superior category.

[1] This psychic body is called *sûkshma śarîra*, and is made of three sheaths: the cognitional (*vijnânamayakośa*), the sensorial (*manamayakośa*), the respiratory (*prâṇamayakośa*). Cf. Jacob, *Hindu Pantheism*, pp. 68–67.

[2] Crozier's *History of Intellectual Development*, p. 86. The author adds: "That in these Hindu philosophies Soul must mean something of this kind would, on reflection, be evident, if from nothing else, from this fact alone, viz., that all their systems, in which it is the object of the individual to unite with the Universal Soul, require for their logical harmony and completeness some scheme of transmigration and re-incarnation after death."

All life is one. Between human and animal on the one side, and human and Divine on the other, as also between human and insentient, there is no impassable gulf fixed. The soul may crawl as a snake, bloom as a flower, roam as a tiger, writhe like a demon, or reign as a god. No embodiment is incongruous or impossible. The whole universe is a collection of abodes, each prepared to offer temporary accommodation to some vagrant soul that has been pursuing its way from times eternal, and must continue to wander through ages incalculable. In that pilgrimage the soul passes through many climates, occupies strangely contrasted homes, lives through the most bewilderingly diversified experiences. Now it is the hunter, then it is the prey. Here it is the criminal, there it is the victim of the crime. Now it aspires to the Divine, then it glories in the bestial, and anon it is aflame with devilry. At one time it emerges into paradise, then it plunges into purgatory.

> Who toiled a slave may come anew a Prince
>   For gentle worthiness and merit won;
> Who ruled a King may wander earth in rags
>   For things done and undone.
>
> Higher than Indra's you may lift your lot,
>   And sink it lower than the worm or gnat;
> The end of many myriad lives is this,
>   The end of myriads that.[1]

But every condition is transitory. If the soul reaches anywhere and at any time a happy embodiment, and says within itself: "Here would I abide"—even while it speaks the wheel turns, and it is projected into another. Hell is temporary, but not less so is heaven. Into

[1] *The Light of Asia.*

whatever state I am born, I am born only to die; but that does not mean rest, for I die only to be born. It is a weary see-saw—arriving but to depart, departing but to return. How long this has gone on I do not know. How much longer it must continue I cannot tell.

> Only, while turns the wheel invisible,
> No pause, no peace, no staying place can be;
> Who mounts may fall, who falls will mount; the spokes
> Go round unceasingly.[1]

The sages speak of "the eighty-four." Nobody can tell how they make their calculation. I only know they mean eighty-four lakhs of births—eight million four hundred thousand! What a prospect, for me or for any one! If only the pilgrimage could be seen to lead anywhere! If it would surely, however slowly, carry us forward and upward! But there is no assurance. Nothing appears but infinite uncertainty. Souls are continually transgressing what seemed to be their category, leaping from deity to devil, being precipitated from sentient to insentient.[2]

II

Is there, then, no clear law determining for us the sequence of our births? "There is," says the Hindu, "and that law is *Karma*." But what is Karma? The word means "action," that which has been done;[3] and

[1] *The Light of Asia.*

[2] *Brihadâranyaka-Upanishad*, VI. ii. 16; *Mundaka Up.* I. ii. 10.

[3] The Karma—all that total of a Soul
Which is the things it did, the thoughts it had,
The 'self' it wove—with woof of viewless time,
Crossed on the warp of invisible acts—
The outcome of him on the Universe.—EDWIN ARNOLD.

the doctrine that it enfolds is this—*the deed determines the destiny.* It is the Hindu's way of saying, and saying with terrific emphasis, what the New Testament also tells us—"Whatsoever a man soweth, that shall he also reap." But he says it with a difference. In attributing everything that is or happens to the predetermining power of Karma, he does not in the least mean to indicate a method of moral government ordained by the sovereign and righteous will of God. He is rather enunciating a law of subjective necessity which determines absolutely and inexorably not only the events, but also *the bias* of every life that appears. Karma is regarded as the ethical expression, by anticipation, of that fundamental law which we now know as the Persistence of Force. No deed is lost. It may be forgotten. Its effects may not begin to manifest themselves at once, or for a long time. But it has created a new energy of merit or demerit which some time, some how, but quite inevitably, will work itself out in the history of the soul. In the embodiment which may come to us at any given change,[1] in the events and environment of that embodiment, in the temper and capacity which we exhibit in it, there is nothing haphazard. My Karma—that which I have been and done in times unremembered—has determined all with absolute precision. However perplexed I may be at that which befalls me, I am to resolve my perplexity by remembering that all this stream of experiences has its origin and strength in the reservoir of my accumulated works.

[1] "It is through the Karma of the past that the individual entity is attracted to the human couple whose heredity and surroundings offer the required conditions to carry on the development from lower to higher." —*Idea of Re-Birth* by F. Arundale.

Whatever my lot, therefore, it is *self-created.* "What living creature slays or is slain? What living creature destroys or is preserved? Each is his own destroyer or preserver, as he follows evil or good." My caste, my country, my increase, my decrease, the gladness that makes me dance, the sorrow that swims my eyes—all are alike in this, that I have somehow shaped them for myself. The garment of circumstance which at any moment I happen to wear, be it coarse and chafing, or a comfort and an adornment, has been woven by my own hands, and I cannot decline to wear it. I have by my own deed enthroned a power which I cannot see, but from which I cannot escape. It is impossible to define it, but it is equally impossible to defeat it.

> *Ye suffer from yourselves.* None else compels,
> None other holds you that ye live and die,
> And whirl upon the wheel, and hug and kiss
> Its spokes of agony,
> Its tire of tears, its nave of nothingness.

The unerring certainty with which Karma works is a topic to which Indian literature of all grades recurs continually. "As among a thousand cows a calf will find its mother, so the deed previously done will find and follow its doer." So says the *Mahâbhârata.* The idea has crystallised itself into one word—*Adṛishṭa*, a word which is very frequently on the lips of Hindus, and is the popular synonym for Karma. It means "the unseen," which is believed to shadow us everywhere, control us always. This has been strikingly expressed in the same epic, the *Mahâbhârata*, thus:—

> Yes, all the deeds that men have done,
> In light of day, before the sun,

> Or veiled beneath the gloom of night,
> The good, the bad, the wrong, the right—
> These, though forgotten, reappear,
> *And travel, silent, in their rear.*

Thus Karma is made to explain all and determine all. Action, whether good or bad, compels a new embodiment, in which the bad may be punished and the good rewarded; and as we cannot live and not act, the weary pilgrim sees not where his wandering is to end. At no period can the soul repose assured. "The very merit that wins a sojourn in paradise or the rank of a divinity must sooner or later be exhausted, and the bankrupt soul descend to a lower sphere."[1] Whither, then, at last? Is there, perchance, a last? Is there anywhere a final home, where the wanderer may find "sleepe after toyle, port after stormie seas, ease after warre"? If so, where is it and how may it be reached? And is there, possibly, a short cut to that home? These are questions which have goaded India into speculation. How could it be otherwise? They appeal to every single Hindu who has ever known pain, or sorrow, or disappointment, with a directness and urgency that are simply irresistible.

But apart altogether from the personal interest which these doctrines compel, there is that in them which challenges the most earnest attention of men of larger view, philosophers and all who try to find the heart of things and see them as a whole. For Karma, it is taught, regulates not only the destiny of the individual, but the origin and development of everything in the world. It is the key to the Hindu's *Weltanschauung*—it is here he begins his

[1] Gough's *Philosophy of the Upanishads*, p. 22.

interpretation of the universe. All the operations of nature are, in his reckoning, the results of the good or bad deeds of the aggregate of souls performed in their various embodiments. The periodic dissolution and reconstitution of worlds is, on the grand scale, analogous to the death and re-birth of individual souls, and is to be accounted for in the same way.[1] In a sense of his own the Hindu uses Paul's words, and tells us that " the whole creation," driven by Karma through successive changes, finding no respite and knowing no rest, " groaneth and travaileth in pain with us " [2]—waiting for deliverance.

Birth and death, death and birth—this is to the Hindu the fugue of the Universe ; often dismal, sometimes maddening, and to all common seeming eternal.

III.

Wherein, then, lies the attraction of such a theory? Well, it is claimed for it that it " rebuilds content with the universe," and dismisses for ever the ghastly nightmare of a predominant injustice. Things may be bad and cruel, but with this hypothesis they are, at least, no longer confusing. The world may be " red in tooth and claw with ravine," but at any rate law is working everywhere, intelligibly and with precision. In spite of all appearances, men are not really the hapless sport of some " Sultan in the sky," whose mood dictates his measures and who is alike incalculable and irresponsible. So, though our lot be misfortune and bitterness, there is no longer added the tormenting suspicion of a chronic injustice. For the first and

[1] Cf. *Sanskrit Literature*, pp. 388, 389.
[2] Romans viii. 22 (R.V. margin).

highest claim of the hypothesis to credit is this—that it substitutes the patient impersonal processes of law, which admit neither of partiality nor error, for the uncertainty and hazard of justice by personal volition. This Karmic justice, once postulated, is made to do its work with the most uncompromising thoroughness. "For stealing grain a man becomes a rat . . . for stealing honey a stinging insect . . . for stealing meat a vulture."[1] Such is the grotesque penal code promulgated by Manu, and there is much more like it. He who is cruel in this birth will appear as a tiger in the next; who steals a horse, wishing to go faster than he ought, will next time be born lame, unable to go as fast as he would; who purloins perfumes now must reappear as a musk rat, more odorous than he desires. Now all this, however fantastic in expression, is at least clear and unassailable in principle. It is the strong affirmation of justice at the heart of things—a justice that never errs and never fails. If it be true, we are told, "puzzledom" is at end, and resignation becomes easy. It may be so. We are at present simply putting the case of those who accept the hypothesis. They are "consoled" to think that no suffering falls unearned. They seem to think that acquiescence is easier if the whipped victim can be assured that, though he does not remember it, he really did at some time or another commit a crime.

But the transmigration doctrine has another attraction. It is claimed for it that it not only rehabilitates Justice but also finally enthrones Hope. It is held to imply the promise that spirit must ultimately conquer matter and all the evil that clings to it. The journey may be long and weary, the

[1] *Laws of Manu*, xii. 62, 63, 65.

ebbs may seem as frequent as the tides, but some where, some time, the spirit will work itself free, and escape its last tenement to greet its source in eternal union. Through whatever stress of pain and change and conflict, however prolonged, every soul is to win the goal at last. There is to be, in the end, no hopeless straggler, none that finally misses his way. Every life in the world, however meanly embodied and however far from the goal, is permitted on this hypothesis to say within itself—

> I shall arrive! What time, what circuit first,
> I ask not.[1]

Transmigration is therefore a doctrine of universal restoration—of restoration, professedly, by long slow purgation. Hindus sometimes contrast this with the Christian teaching of "eternal sin." To them, they say, that doctrine means the defeat of God. That all men should at last, far off, be saved—that, they tell us, would be to the eternal glory of God. Or that God should crush out of His universe those who are finally impenitent and incorrigible, and then reign for ever supreme and unchallenged Lord—*that*, they say, would be intelligible and not unreasonable. But that there should be a section of God's creatures who will not yield in love nor bow in fear, who obey only under compulsion and shriek out defiance even while they obey—that they regard as an abhorrent view, committing men to the anticipation of an eternal discord in the music of the spheres. A consideration like this, while it serves the Hindu in passing argument, is eagerly fastened upon and strongly emphasised by many in Europe.

But what, we may ask, is the value of the "salvation"

[1] Browning, *Paracelsus*.

procured by such a process as transmigration? From beginning to end it is purely automatic—as mechanical, apparently, as the gradual metamorphosis of the caterpillar into the butterfly. Nothing could be more interesting, and the result is beautiful, but it is all so inevitable that no one dreams of giving credit for its evolution to any individual insect. If of two caterpillars one performs its journey to the perfected butterfly-stage sooner than the other, who applauds the winner or condemns the laggard? So it is, also, in the more elaborate metamorphosis of the soul. If human will enters into the matter at all, the only effect it can have is to hasten or retard, perhaps by an æon or two, perhaps only by a century or two, the final emergence of the soul. Sooner or later the end is completely assured.

> The firm soul hastes, the feeble tarries. ALL
> *Will reach the sunlit snows.*

Whatever the soul's relation to God, and we may add, whatever God's attitude to the soul, the process works itself through at last inevitably, and the "individualised spirit" is merged into Universal Being. If this be so, there is nothing worth while left for man to do. He is simply the victim of a great cosmic process, and the destined end will come whatever he does or does not, and whether he desires or protests. Still less, however, is there for God to do. If the doctrine of "eternal sin" means the defeat of God, that of transmigration apparently means His dismissal.[1] That, indeed, with many who hold this

[1] Macdonell remarks quite justly that "there is no room for independent divine rule by the side of the power of Karma, which governs everything with iron necessity."—*Sanskrit Literature*, p. 389.

doctrine, is what it comes to. Buddha frankly faced that result and acquiesced in it, and in this respect he is generally followed by present-day Theosophists in Europe. God deposed and man discrowned—that is what transmigration, with all its promise of universal restoration, really brings us to. If it leaves God at all to the world, as Hindus would insist that it does, it leaves Him only as a distant, silent, uninterfering and practically uninterested Observer of the processes which, perchance, He instituted, but which He has no power either to change or arrest. And if it gives to man any dignity whatsoever above insentient atoms, it does so by crediting him with the merest shred and semblance of freedom, the possession of which does not, in the sum of things, really matter at all. Christianity, on the other hand, when it speaks of "eternal sin," assumes that man is made in the image of God, and is therefore endowed in measure with that freedom which is a necessary attribute of the Personal Creator. Such freedom may be used in obedience. But it may also be misused in disobedience; in which case (if the soul is immortal, as Hindus believe with us, and if God will not "overpower and annihilate that gift of freedom which makes us men"), eternal defiance of God and final disunion from Him are not only possible to contemplation, but may be realised in fact.

IV

Let us now turn to a critical examination of this hypothesis.

1. To begin with, it is neither proved nor provable, and it bases itself, besides, on a totally inadmissible assump-

tion. That assumption is the pre-existence of the soul. The idea is one which finds neither analogy nor other confirmation in experience, but it has nevertheless been an interest and allurement both to the poets and philosophers of Europe through many ages. In India, however, the notion is fundamental. Without it not only would transmigration disappear, but the hope of immortality would seem to become insecure. For it is an axiom with the Hindu, that *that which has had a beginning must*, ipso facto, *have an end*, and he is bound to maintain, therefore, that if the soul did not exist before, and exist *always*, it must inevitably die. This dictum has travelled to Europe and been used by many, Immanuel Fichte among others, in vindication of the doctrine of immortality. There can be no better answer to it than that which has been given by Dr. Martineau. He admits its truth within the limits of organic life, "whose history consists of a cycle of chemical changes"; but he denies that it holds in other spheres. Newton's first law, for instance, declares that a particle once set in motion in empty space will continue to move in a straight line with uniform velocity *for ever*, unless some external force supervenes. Clearly the dictum cannot hold there. Why should it hold, then, in spheres intellectual and moral any more than in spheres mechanical? May not a spiritual nature, once set up by God out of the resources of His own being, endure as long as the God in whom it lives? "So far as thought and love and goodness are related to Time, their relation is not cyclical, but progressive; not returning to their beginnings, but opening out into indefinite enlargement and acceleration. The dictum, therefore, that what begins must end is one to which we are not bound to surrender; and the only pre-existence which we need allow to the soul is latent within its Divine Source, ere yet its idea has taken effect and the personal monad been set up."[1]

That which would best prove pre-existence is just that which is never available—recollection. Nor is it unreasonable to ask for it. It is impossible to conceive of identity of subject amid changing experiences without crediting the subject with continuity and coherence; and the faculty which above all others is needed to certify that continuity is memory. But it is just here that advocates of the hypothesis are most hopelessly baffled. They have clutched at any straw which would help them. East and West the intuitions of childhood have been interpreted as "shadowy recollections"; but this is confessedly a suggestion so tentative and unsubstantiated that nothing can be built on it. The Hindus have ventured further. They tell us that some of the ancient sages and saints of their race could recall previous births distinctly, and they maintain that even now, if pious austerities be persisted in, the recollection may once more be recovered. In the meantime no one has it or professes to have it; nor does any one now living recall any others who ever had it. Forgotten experiences have a wonderful way of flashing back upon the recollection—in delirium, in drowning, at times of sudden nervous shock. In the palimpsest of memory, events that had long been hopelessly over-written have, as in a moment, become suddenly decipherable; but every recovered recollection has to do only with this one life of ours on earth. The bridge which should connect this life

[1] *A Study of Religion*, vol. ii. p. 334.

in our consciousness with a previous one is finally swept away; not a stone or stick of it remains. This does not, by itself, disprove the doctrine; but if that which is otherwise alleged in support of it is unsatisfactory, then the fact that *no one remembers* is sufficient to conclude its condemnation.

2. Moreover, the fact that no one remembers has this grave consequence—*it entirely voids the doctrine of moral purpose and utility.* When the element of recollection is absent, and no positive evidence of any other kind is forthcoming, the prisoner is, for purposes of justice, no longer identical with the criminal. That which I suffer at any time is, in the absence of memory, not penalty, but simply misfortune; that which I enjoy is not reward, but sheer good luck. In these circumstances, my sufferings may properly arouse within me regret, or resentment, or resignation—anything, indeed, but repentance. To my conscience they make no appeal whatsoever. They do not compel a sense of guilt, for the soul knows nothing of which it can be said to be guilty. Bitterness and bewilderment may both arise—but not self-blame. And as my sufferings convey no reproof, so of course they suggest no reform. Whatever else may be said for transmigration, it cannot properly be said that it is "a reformatory discipline." The quality of our present experience does not help us to determine the class of deeds out of which it has arisen, and therefore provides neither warning nor incentive. We are all "homeless, wandering ghosts whom death is constantly dislodging." As we leave one abode we pass through the waters of Lethe and enter the next, bringing with us no guidance whatever from all our past experience.

No conceivable arrangement could seem more purposeless, none more wasteful. It cuts right athwart all the economies of nature, as science has taught us to observe them. Nature does not habitually perpetuate results, while yet carefully obliterating all remembrance or other indication of their causes. It is because we can, with increasing assurance, connect the two that knowledge grows and progress is possible. But with the transmigration hypothesis we face the results of the past without any key to unlock their meaning. They *have* no meaning, therefore. No patience or industry or ingenuity can force from our previous history even a hint to help us in interpreting the situation that confronts us now. The story through which we lived in the last embodiment is lost. If it had a moral, that, too, is forgotten. In this birth we have opened a new volume which no reading of any previous one can help us to understand. The entail of the past is with us—so much we know; but what its value is and how to treat it we are simply denied all means of knowing. So, if this scheme of successive births and deaths be evolution, it is purely natural and mechanical; it is quite certain that there is nothing moral about it.

3. The general sense of the people has construed this doctrine aright. They trace their present sufferings, not to fault, but to fate. Karma has produced their present, and, as I have shown, Karma is simply "doing." But what did they, and under what compulsion? They may have "done," but they know of no responsibility for it; they have no belief that they could have avoided doing it. It was doubtless a necessitated act; necessitated, if not by constraint from without, then by impulsion from

within. Anyhow, that determined this. They are simply the victims, therefore, of a past which they do not remember, but from which they cannot escape—a past which dictates the present, and thus prepares the future quite beyond their power to challenge and alter it. What, then, lies within their power? They feel no responsibility, for they know of no choice. "At any given moment of their life their next action is by hypothesis strictly determined."[1] Their destiny has long since, and without any consultation of them, passed out of their control. So, when a Hindu loses a limb, he submits in uncomplaining acquiescence, with the remark—"It is my fate." But he surrenders his purity also, or his honesty, and finds refuge in the same defence—"It is my fate." Bad or good, sad or glad, the developments of life are to him, because of this doctrine, inevitable and irreversible; and so reform is ruled out of his creed, and hope (so far as the present embodiment is concerned) omitted from his vocabulary.

4. But there are other difficulties in transmigration. *Consider, for instance, the account that it gives of suffering.* According to its interpretation, suffering is always penal. In whatever form it comes it is to be regarded as the outworking of demerit. Such a theory takes us back to the days of Job, and makes every sorrow that befalls a man God's branding of a criminal, the infallible token that He has a controversy with him. But how does this hold? Surely it is the noblest lives that have ever been the saddest. Sainthood and sorrow have been so persistently associated as to be almost synonymous. A fine spiritual nature always isolates a man. A strongly developed

[1] Balfour's *Foundations of Belief*, p. 147.

moral sense makes him the constant target of misinterpretation and maltreatment. The highest forms of excellence, like the topmost peaks in mountain ranges, are oftenest wrapped in thick cloud, and round them rage the fiercest storms. How comes it, on the transmigration theory, that in the same embodiment, character and circumstance should be in such tragic contradiction—

> Truth for ever on the scaffold,
> Wrong for ever on the throne?

How are we to construe the great martyrdoms of history—martyrdoms endured in the interests of science, good government, or religion? Are we to say that the noble qualities—courage and self-forgetting devotion to truth—which these martyrs exhibited were consequent on the merit acquired in a former birth, while their sufferings and untimely death were the punishment due to demerit? But their sufferings were self-chosen, and in the choice their moral greatness most revealed itself. When Moses made his great refusal, when holy women surrendered themselves unhesitatingly to torture and death, "not accepting deliverance," human nature was scaling its highest summits. Yet their heroic devotion brought them the sharpest suffering; they had to encounter ignominy, deprivation, injustice, in their cruellest form. But there is one supreme example before which all others pale. What, on the theory we are considering, are we to say of Christ, in Whom by universal confession dwelt all divine qualities perfectly, and Who nevertheless had to endure the Cross? Was He, in the sorrows and humiliations of His life, and in the circumstances of His death, merely the driven victim of some fearful unremembered demerit? Are we to suppose that in a former embodiment He combined the most unsullied goodness and the most unqualified badness, and that in this birth they bore their appropriate fruit in a divine nature set in surroundings of hellish suffering? Would not one set of qualities, then, have limited, or perhaps even annulled, the other set? Could angel and demon have dwelt together in the same home, neither seeking to eject or even to pinion the other? At the very least, might we not expect that previous merit would have modified the misery, and previous demerit have dimmed the lustre of character, of Him who stands before the world peerless alike in goodness and in grief? "Once for all the sinless suffering of the Cross parted sin from suffering with a clearness of distinction" which can never again be obscured, and in that distinction transmigration as a theory of suffering stands finally discredited. In very truth no interpretation could be more harsh and narrow, or less intelligent.

Sin always has issue in pain and need and sorrow, but where these are found it does not always follow that there also has been sin. Christianity recognises that suffering, however mysterious and however painful, is good in meaning and often most noble in result. "Even more than knowledge, pain is power,"[1] and develops the latent capacity of our being as no other influence can. It is not only a corrective force, but it is also preventive and stimulating. "The pleasures of each generation evaporate in air; it is their pains that increase the spiritual momentum of the world."[2] It is simple truth to say

[1] *Lux Mundi*, p. 118. [2] *Ibid.* p. 124.

that the noblest qualities of humanity, courage, patience, tenderness, unselfishness, have reached their highest development through suffering; that the impulse towards progress, whether in science, or literature, or morals, or government, has been born of disappointment, dissatisfaction, and need; that the world's best possessions, freedom, security, health, knowledge, spiritual comfort and material resource, have become ours at the cost of "broken hearts, tired brains, and many noble lives laid down." Thus we see that suffering, instead of being merely a sign of penalty, is frequently, perhaps generally, the spring of progress. "Its absence would mean stagnation, quiescence, unprogressiveness."[1] And when God would lead humanity to its highest developments, He sent forth Jesus, "the Man of Sorrows," "to taste death for every man." In that sacrifice Jesus Christ summed up all lower analogies, all humbler examples, and through Calvary made a way for all men unto the Father.

5. Transmigration finds the explanation of the inequalities of birth and the sorrows of experience in individual demerit. There, in its view, is the final cause, and every other explanation merely points to an intermediate agency. Yet some of these explanations are weighty, and, as far as they go, beyond challenge. It is unquestioned, for instance, that many of the ills from which we suffer have been directly transmitted to us from our ancestors. Consumption in one, unstable mental equilibrium in another, criminal bias in a third—these are admittedly the undesirable bestowals of predecessors, and would seem to be in no just sense chargeable to the

[1] Fiske's *Through Nature to God*, p. 54.

present sufferers. But we are told that, though this account is scientific, yet science can deal only with obvious and immediate processes, not with ultimate controlling causes. Transmigration assumes that the body is not organic to the soul any more than the cell is to the prisoner or the night shelter to the wanderer. In the case of consumptives or criminals, or any of those to whom heredity seems to have brought misfortune, what really happened, we are told, was this: the parents provided the physical conditions suitable to the demerit of some waiting disembodied entity which was thereby "attracted," and so came to its present unhappy embodiment! This is gruesome teaching. If it were true, then nobody need have any concern as to the conditions of reproduction. Idiots, diseased, criminal may multiply at will. They are simply providing appropriate penal habitations for waiting sinful souls. All those costly devices by which philanthropy seeks to limit and defeat the results of evil heredity, are simply a gratuitous interference with the workings of Karmic law! If transmigration be true, men may not blame those who came before them, and they owe nothing to those who will come after them. Each person exists for himself alone. Others have no necessary interest in him and no true hold upon him. The solidarity of the race is a fiction, and *individualism is the supreme law.*[1]

[1] This is well illustrated by the notion so prevalent among Hindus, that a man is responsible only for his personal conduct, and has no responsibility for the general system of things as it exists around him. On this point, cf. Mr. Meredith Townsend's *Asia and Europe*, p. 143. See also a very interesting paragraph on Individualism in Findlay's *Christian Doctrine and Morals*, p. 158, which I met with after the text had been written.

Each soul is a solitary wanderer which alights here or there as its Karma may determine, but it bears no vital relation to the parents who have supplied the shell in which, for the time being, it has found accommodation for itself. Thus on this theory parentage is only physical, and the essential man has had no father and will have no son!

But besides heredity there are other causes of pain and misfortune. A careless nurse, for instance, spills boiling water over her charge and scalds it within an inch of its life; or an engine-driver, having drunk too freely, neglects a signal, and thereby permanently cripples half a train-load of passengers. In these cases it is obvious to explain the trouble by the carelessness of one person and the criminal self-indulgence of the other. But the transmigration theory cannot be satisfied with this. It asks the question—Why should it have been *that* child that was in the nurse's hands rather than another? Why should *those* people have been injured in the railway accident rather than any others? "Why, indeed," it answers, "except that in this way their unknown Karma was working out its proper and necessary results?" There was therefore no accident, and careless nurse and drunken driver were the appointed though unwitting ministers of justice! It may seem revolting that such a conclusion should be possible, but so indeed it stands. Press the notion to its proper conclusion, and again it would appear that the whole system of checks and penalties by which society protects itself is a calculated interference with the working of Karmic law!

But even supposing that transmigration has its way, and that in the interests of ideal justice we trace back all suffering to individual demerit, we are not therefore at the end of our difficulties. How came there, in the first instance, to be demerit at all? We are forbidden to suppose that for some inscrutable reason it was permitted by a supreme Personal Will. That, we are told, would be to introduce "caprice" into the government of the universe. On the transmigration theory, demerit must be postulated as inherent in the universe. With this postulate granted, men cease to talk of misfortune and all other calamity as "injustice," and reckon it merely the appropriate penalty for sin whose beginning remains unexplained. But this is a mere playing with words. Transmigration does not lighten the central darkness by a single gleam. The truth is, we are all bound to allow that moral evil is an ultimate fact beyond denial, even if not wholly beyond explanation. The one practical problem is how, moral evil being in the world, character may be saved from extinction thereby, and even trained to strength and perfect purity. In that process pain in all its forms plays an essential and beneficent part. Trial develops strength, grief is the pathway to higher joy, outward impoverishment leads to inner enrichment, loss of position to the gain of manhood. *Via crucis via lucis*, is written large all through human history, and to trace back all suffering to individual demerit is to perpetrate an anticlimax which is as paralysing as it is absurd.

6. There is still another point upon which we must touch briefly. Transmigration, as we have seen, is a theory of relentless justice. What I have sowed, that—not more, but never less, and never otherwise—must I reap. Now,

such a theory works in two ways. (*a*) *It checks and almost entirely excludes pity for others.* If I see a man in trouble, what is that to me? He ran up a bill some time or other in a previous birth, and he is now painfully paying off his score. It is no concern of mine. He incurred the debt without consulting me, and he must just settle it by himself. I have my own bill to settle, and that gives me quite enough to do without my troubling about any one else's. That, as a matter of fact, is exactly the spirit which has been induced in the people of India by this doctrine. If, for instance, a little girl is bereft of the man to whom she was betrothed, it is inferred that her sin is finding her out, and her people emphasise the inference by all sorts of neglect and social degradation. The same thing runs right through. Let come what will, it is all earned, they say; then why should they build hospitals for the sick, or found charities for the poor? They curse the man whom circumstances seem to curse, even as they fawn before the man whom circumstances seem to favour. In another way, also, this doctrine brings about the same result. Not only does it proclaim that all a man suffers is deserved, but it also tells us that this life is only one short and not specially important stage in an illimitable journey to the Infinite. Why, then, should we waste pity on any one? His lot may be miserable, but after all it is only a brief uncomfortable half-hour in æons upon æons of existence. The doctrine effectually "extinguishes human sympathy for the individual by minimising the importance of a single life."[1] It is no wonder that Mr. Meredith Townsend is found

[1] Lyall's *Asiatic Studies*, Second Series, p. 14.

declaring, though in a different connection, that "in Asia . . . sympathy has yet to be born."[1] Pity has poor chance where transmigration holds.

(*b*) But, further, it leaves no room for betterment *and bars all hope of forgiveness.* Forgiveness? That word lies quite outside its vocabulary. Karma never errs, but also it never spares. "It knows not wrath *nor pardon.*" Penalty follows sin in inexorable sequence. Nemesis, if not swift, is always sure, and absolutely uncompromising. Nothing can arrest it, nothing mitigate it. Repentance is useless, resentment irrational, escape impossible.

> The Moving Finger writes; and, having writ,
> Moves on; nor all your Piety and Wit
> Shall lure it back to cancel half a Line,
> Nor all your Tears wash out a Word of it.[2]

God stands without, witnessing the movement of this fearful engine, but never seeking to deflect its course by a single hair's breadth; untouched by pity, unconcerned for character, indifferent to the increase of righteousness—content that justice shall have its perfect work. If such be the system under which we live, if we are simply the victims of a mighty cosmic process, then he mocks who talks of forgiveness. The sinner is moving towards a midnight that can never be followed by a morning. There are no stars in his sky, and he hears no music but the dirge of doom.

But though natural law is inflexible and contains within itself no single hint of forgiveness, we are familiar enough with the idea when we come into the region of

[1] *Asia and Europe*, p. 264.
[2] Edward Fitzgerald's *Omar Khayyám*, lxxi.

personality. In human society forgiveness is every day needed and every day granted; and if we can be assured of a God who is personal, governed by personal qualities and exercising personal relations, forgiveness of sin at once becomes conceivable. Now, such in fact is the conception of God presented to us in the Bible. He is described to us, for instance, as "the LORD, the LORD, a God full of compassion and gracious, slow to anger and plenteous in mercy and truth; keeping mercy for thousands, forgiving iniquity, transgression, and sin; and that will by no means clear the guilty."[1]

So, then, the personal God does not discredit and discard the law of retributive justice. He is a righteous God, who "will not clear the guilty." He does not palter with evil. He is unalterably opposed to it. The law of retribution which finds expression in the nature of things is *His* law, ordained by Him in token that He is eternally intolerant of wrong, that He will pursue it unfalteringly, and condemn it unsparingly. By no act can He ever palliate sin or make light of it. He hates it with unsleeping and undying hate. But God is a Father, and the sinner is His child; and the child is as precious to Him as the sin is hateful. He would crush that, but would save him. He has made men in His image and for His fellowship, and He cannot be satisfied that they should be spoiled and lost to Him until His love has used all righteous means to fetch them home. He is the God of grace as well as of law. Love is as natural to Him as holiness, and mercy is as essentially His attribute as justice. The two are not in antagonism, but work towards

[1] Exodus xxxiv. 6, 7 (R. V.).

the same end. In order to save the sinner, He must be relentlessly hostile to the sin. The measure of His love to the man will be the measure of His loathing for the sin. He cannot undo it, and He may not ignore it; but He may, on conditions, forgive it. Forgiveness is always conditioned. Where the offence is purely personal and private, there must at least be regret, the willingness if possible to make amends, and the implied resolve not to repeat it. As between man and man this is frequently enough, and the old relations of regard and confidence are readily resumed. But where the offence touches not only personal relations but the public weal, where the person offended is not merely the father of the offender but the Sovereign of the State whose laws have been outraged, then it is conceivable that, with the forgiveness which restores the original relations between father and son, there may yet be dealt out such measure of punishment as shall vindicate the law and deter others from violating it. As between God and His children, this, we are told, is exactly what happens. "Thou wast a God that forgavest them," says the Psalmist, "and tookest vengeance of their doings."[1] Forgiveness is not the instant and undiscriminating abrogation of all penalty. It *must* mean the reversal of relations between God and the sinner, and with that the end of separation, which is the chief and deadliest element in sin's penalty. But there are secondary and less vital consequences of sin which will still run their course even when forgiveness has taken place. The health wasted by vice may never be wholly restored; the fortune squandered in self-indulgence may never be

[1] Psalm xcix. 8.

recovered; the damaged reputation may never be perfectly rehabilitated. Pardon may be blended with punishment, mercy may consist with suffering, and the love of the Father effect its purpose while yet the righteous Sovereign guards the public weal. But the changed relations between God and the sinner at once begin to react upon the sinner's view of those natural penalties which still continue. He begins to see them from his Father's point of view. They are a standing reminder to him, alike of his shame and of the mercy that will reckon it against him no more for ever.

This forgiveness God has made possible in Christ Jesus. "God was in Christ reconciling the world unto Himself."[1] The plan of redemption began with Him, and it was carried out by Christ, His Son and the strong Head and eternal Representative of our race, as willingly as obediently. Man's plight was fearful. He was not only ensnared by evil, but enamoured of it. Then stood forth Christ, our sinless Brother, acknowledging to the full His relationship to us, while yet in all things one with God. On the one hand, the Father's purpose of mercy was His purpose, and the Father's essential attachment to righteousness wrought in Him also with perfect strength; while, on the other hand, He accepted the full obligation of His unique relation to humanity. It was thus that He waged on our behalf God's conflict against evil. For us He bore the brunt of the battle and received the cruellest blows; for us He rendered that full satisfaction to outraged law which we could not render and live; for us He made that perfect submission to righteousness of which we, on our own initiative, had become morally incapable. And He

[1] 2 Cor. v. 19.

did all this of perfect right, in virtue of His position as Head and Leader of our race. There is no sneer so frequent, but none also so cheap and shallow, as the sneer at vicarious suffering. We are not human islands, each for himself and by himself. We are parts of a mighty organism, each bound by vital and indissoluble ties to the other, and all to Christ. The good that comes to us, and not less the evil, comes to us vicariously. It is because others have fought that we are free; it is because others have toiled that we are wise; and our good and evil are working blessing and suffering for others. "The vicarious principle, the representative office held by man for his fellow-man, is of the essence of morality, and binds mankind into its ethical unity."[1] That principle finds its most perfect illustration in the work which Christ did when He came "not to be ministered unto but to minister, and to give His life a ransom for many."[2] That which He did was right for Him and necessary for us; the supreme affirmation of the Father's love and holiness and of His own living headship of our race. "The chastisement of our peace was upon Him, and with His stripes we are healed."[3] As we associate ourselves by faith with Him, and, realising all that sin has done, turn away from it with loathing and fear, the relationship which had been broken is renewed, and the sin which separated between us and our God is "blotted out as a cloud." This gospel of forgiveness turns midnight into morning, and brings back to human life love for fear, joy for sorrow, and hope for despair.

[1] Findlay's *Christian Doctrine and Morals*, p. 158.
[2] Matt. xx. 28.
[3] Isaiah liii. 5.

PART II

Hindu Pantheism

"I am God, and there is none else."—ISAIAH xlv. 22.

"Hear, O Israel: the Lord our God is one Lord."—DEUT. vi. 4.

"Brahma is true; the world is false; the soul is Brahma himself, and nothing other."—VEDÂNTIC TEXT (origin unknown).

"Brahma alone—a spirit; essentially existent, intelligence, and joy; void of all qualities and of all acts; in whom there is no consciousness such as is denoted by 'I,' 'thou,' and 'it'; who apprehends no person, or thing, nor is apprehended of any; who is neither parviscient nor omniscient; neither parvipotent nor omnipotent; who has neither beginning nor end; immutable and indefectible—is the true entity. All besides himself, the entire universe, is false, that is to say, is nothing whatsoever. Neither has it ever existed, nor does it now exist, nor will it exist at any time future. And the soul is one with Brahma."—SUMMARY OF VEDÂNTIC TEACHING BY NEHEMIAH NI'LAKANTHA S'A'STRI' GORE.

"So God created man in His own image, in the image of God created He him."—GEN. i. 27.

"He that planted the ear, shall He not hear? He that formed the eye, shall He not see?"—PSALM xciv. 9.

"Personality, with all its limitations, though far from exhibiting the absolute nature of God as He is, is yet truer, grander, and more elevating, more religious, than those barren, vague, meaningless abstractions in which men babble about nothing under the name of the Infinite."—MANSEL'S *Bampton Lectures*, p. 61.

"One God, one law, one element,
And one far-off Divine event,
To which the whole creation moves."—
TENNYSON'S *In Memoriam*.

SECTION I

FOREST MEDITATIONS

There he kept
In solitude and solitary thought
His mind in a just equipoise of love.
Serene it was, unclouded by the cares
Of ordinary life; unvexed, unwarped
By partial bondage.—WORDSWORTH.

THE most stirring consciousness of the old thinkers of India was, as we have seen, that of transiency and suffering. There is no effect without a cause, and every effect becomes itself a new cause. We are here now because we suffered and wrought elsewhere, and this life will in due time compel another. Where shall it end? Is this to be an eternal itinerancy, and however long and far we travel are we never to be a day's march nearer home? No prospect could be more dismal. If in our present birth suffering is predominant, then the worst has already happened, except that it may be repeated indefinitely; but if perchance our present lot is comparatively happy, the happiness is marred by the conviction that it cannot last. Even though we should reach heaven and rank with gods, yet inevitably and soon there will come a turn of the wheel which will dislodge us and plunge us back again into the weltering vortex below. *Anitya, dukkha, anatta*—impermanence, sorrow, unreality[1]—these are the words with which every day the Buddhist tells his beads and recites his views of life; and though death comes, surely it is still only the portal to another birth. When will the weary treadmill stop? We are always born with desire, desire always provokes action, and action good or bad always has fruit in further embodiment. Where is the state, far-off, in which "the wicked cease from troubling and the weary are at rest"; when desire shall be satisfied or extinguished, and when change, which is caused by desire, shall be at an end.

It was through such questions as these that men were driven to philosophise. There were keen intellects and eager spirits in those days, as there are still, and in India thought has ever been counted greater than action. In the arrangements of life there, while due consideration is given to the practical side of it, and every Brâhman is expected to fulfil the duties of husband, father, and householder, yet it has always been recommended that at some period (say about the age of fifty), he who has hitherto been a man of the world and of affairs should relinquish his position and retire to the forest—there to shut his eyes to all mere passing shows of things, and visualise to himself the Eternal; to have done for ever with appearance, and tread the pathway to reality. There is a special class of literature, the *Âraṇyakas*[2] or "Forest-books," prepared for

[1] Cf. Spence Hardy's *Manual of Buddhism*, p. 288.

[2] The most ancient and sacred books of India are the four Vedas—collections of hymns and prayers, whose composition and compilation probably extended over several hundreds of years. Around these, when they had fully established themselves as books of revelation (*s'ruti*), grew up numerous prose writings called Brâhmaṇas. These contain directions for worship and sacrifice, with expositions of the hymns and mythological

such times and such people—treatises discussing the nature of God and expounding the mystic meaning of religious rites. Connected with these *Âraṇyakas* are the Upanishads, in many ways the most important writings in India, and without a study of which no true comprehension of the history of Indian thought is in the least possible. The word "Upanishad" means, as Max Müller pointed out, "'sitting near a person,' the French *séance* or session." He suggests that these Upanishads "may represent to us the outcome of 'sittings' or 'gatherings' which took place under the shelter of mighty trees in the forest, where old sages and their disciples met together and poured out what they had gathered during days and nights spent in quiet solitude and meditation. . . . Think what their life must have been in these forests, with few cares and fewer ambitions!"[1] A cave on the hillside would give them lodging; the young disciples would procure and prepare the simple meal; and meantime the old sages could think, without haste and without distraction. Then they would gather together their disciples in the gracious cool of the late afternoon, or later still, when the grass was flecked with moonlight, and myriad fire-flies flashed and faded in unhalting rhythm, and glow-worms brought their tiny lamps to grace the session. There the Masters would vocalise their musings, not dogmatically, but tentatively and interrogatively, provoking the young minds around them to suggest a logical doubt or a confirming illustra-

illustrations. The Âraṇyakas are supplementary to the Brâhmaṇas, but of equal authority as revelation. Four of these are extant. To the Âraṇyakas are attached the Upanishads. These form the third great division of the sacred literature of the Brâhmans, and contain their esoteric teaching.

[1] *The Vedânta Philosophy*, pp. 23, 24.

tion; here a qualification, there an expansion. These men had time. This year or next—it did not matter when. They could continue till they were sure. So with infinite patience they elaborated and refined, started objections and pursued them, for the sheer delight of refuting them. It was an admirable method—the thinking of one or two tested, qualified, elaborated, and confirmed by a group. The topics were few in number, but infinite in content. These forest students were but little concerned with popular religion, with gods and sacrifice and all the varied ritual of common worship. Such things belonged to the *karma-mârga*, the way of works, along which the unspiritual and undiscerning made their slow way towards the Infinite. But these things were only superficial and transitory, and they for their part sought the fundamental and the eternal. They were treading the *jnâna-mârga*, the way of knowledge. They wanted to know what they were and whence and why; what the world around them was, alike in its real nature and in its relation to themselves; and above all, what God was. Their thoughts tried many tracks, and they were not easily discouraged; for they were moved to activity and enterprise always by that dismal cycle of change, which in its pitiless sweep comprehended them all.

In all their thinking these men had one common starting-point. Whatever road they meant to travel, they began by subscribing to the infallibility of the Vedas. Hindus have ever believed in revelation, and they have always been one in fighting the denier of it. But there their unity has ended. In interpretation they have been not one but legion, separated by whole hemispheres, yet able to claim legitimacy each for his peculiar doctrine because of his avowed adherence to the Vedas! Pantheist, Deist and Theist in religion, Monist and Dualist, Empiricist and Idealist in philosophy, all discover for themselves hospitality and a welcome inside those sacred pages. But there is one system which, while grounding itself like all the other systems on the Vedas, yet transcends them all, alike in the daring and attractiveness of its speculations, and in the extent and importance of its influence, and that is the system which I would now invite the reader to study. It is called the Vedânta,[1] and professes to set forth the final and essential meaning of the original Hindu Scriptures. It systematises in a series of aphorisms that philosophy which, in unsystematised form, runs right through the numerous Upanishadṣ. The aphorisms have been constructed with a view to being committed to memory, and bear the name of the Vedânta-Sûtras.[2] Their first aim has been conciseness, and everything else—grammar, clearness, force—has been sacrificed to that. The end could scarcely have been more effectively attained, for they are throughout concise to the point of practical unintelligibility. Under these circumstances, it is little wonder that many commentators have been attracted to them.[3] They offer a fine field for intrepid originality. But of all commentators, the greatest, by universal consent, was one whose name is even yet but little known in England. He was called S′ankarâchârya,

[1] Vedânta = the end of the Veda, and may be taken either in the sense of the final portion or ultimate meaning of the Veda.

[2] These Sûtras are ascribed to Bâdarâyaṇa, but no date can be fixed for them with certainty.

[3] Mr. Fitz-Edward Hall speaks of having himself seen fourteen commentaries.

or, in brief, S'ankara. He is said to have been born on the Malabar coast, and to have flourished about the end of the eighth or beginning of the ninth century of our era. He is the leader and representative of the orthodox Vedântists,[1] and his system is one of strict monism, absolute idealism. What Plato was in the philosophy of Greece, what Kant has been in the philosophy of Europe—that, not less, perhaps more, has S'ankara been in the philosophy of India. To his teaching we must now turn.

[1] Next to S'ankara, the most important commentator on the Sûtras was Râmânuja, supposed to have lived in the twelfth century. He strongly opposed the uncompromising monism (*advaita*) of S'ankara, and taught the doctrine of qualified non-duality (*Visis'ṭâdvaita*), with a personal God to Whom man may be assimilated, but with Whom he can never be absolutely identified.

SECTION II

THE IMPERSONAL ONE

Know
He sees indeed who sees in all alike
The living, lordly soul; the soul supreme,
Imperishable amid the Perishing;
For, whoso thus beholds, in every place,
In every form, the same, one, Living Life,
Doth no more wrongfulness unto himself,
But goes the highest road which brings to bliss.
Seeing, he sees indeed, who . . .
. . . sees the mass
Of separate living things—each of its kind—
Issue from One, and blend again to One.
Then hath he Brahma; he attains!—

BHAGAVAD GÎTA, as translated by
SIR EDWIN ARNOLD.

IN this present birth, and, according to the Hindu, in all births, there are at least three marks—transiency, suffering, and manifoldness. From transiency there comes a haunting sense of insecurity; from suffering, misery; from manifoldness, the confusion of error. Plainly, then, the way of relief, if such there be, must lie in substituting permanence for transiency, impassivity for suffering, and unity for manifoldness. But how can this be done? If perchance we could be united with the essential principle of life, then indeed death would cease; if we could find and possess the eternal principle of happiness, then desire and distraction would for ever pass away; if we could discover the ultimate unity, then the possibility of error would disappear. Truth, peace, life—let us find these in their essence, and the storm-tossed boat would be anchored at last in the harbour; the weary and travel-stained pilgrim would be at home.

It was under the inspiration of sentiments like these that the forest sages set forth on their great quest. "Oh, that we might find Him!" was their continual cry; "Him—or is it perhaps That?—which amid universal impermanence abides, which is not driven by desire nor deceived by complexity, which is in all and yet more than all." It was a mighty quest and a determined one. To those men essence was everything, embodiment nothing. They would fain tear down all veils of things and see the thing-in-itself, the Source and Secret of all; they sought the Universal Synthesis, in which all differences should find their final reconciliation; they aimed to touch the Ultimate Reality, which is beyond change and suffering and mistake—the Absolute. Union with That, they said, would surely bring them freedom.

Now this is the point to which the Vedânta philosophy seeks, indeed, to conduct men. Its final revelation to the tired pilgrim lies in this one word—*Tat twam asi*, 'THAT ART THOU.' "There," it has been truly said, "you have the supreme philosophy of India in a nutshell, and all the rest is mere explication." What does this strange text mean—'That art thou'? It is the Hindu way of saying that God and the soul are one—not merely (as the Christian would mean by that phrase) accordant in purpose, combined in effort, and united in affection—but identical. When you have brushed aside all mere guesses, recanted all errors, and cutting through all illusions have reached the last truth, it is this: *Aham Brahmâsmi*—'I am Brahma'; not in part, but absolutely and completely; not through a slow process of approximation, but eternally. That is the fundamental truth, the realisation of which is the Vedântist's heaven. Once that light dawns, the day will never darken more. "What sorrow can there be to him who beholds that unity?" "The fetter of the heart is broken, all doubts are solved."[1] 'I am Brahma.'

Plainly this is not a self-evident truth. My consciousness tells me that I am I, and you are you, and I infer that as I am a separate entity in relation to you, so also am I separate in relation to God. "But that," says the Vedântist, "is the source of all the trouble, and not until you come to yourself as you really are, one with the Absolute, like water in water, fire in fire, ether in ether, the one indistinguishable from the other, can you attain deliverance from the misery of re-incarnations."[2]

[1] *Mundaka-Upanishad*, II. ii. 8.

[2] It has been frequently pointed out how closely religious mysticism in all creeds seems to draw towards the spiritual ideals of Pantheism. But it has not been better stated anywhere than by Professor James. He says:—"This overcoming of all the usual barriers between the individual and the Absolute is the great mystic achievement. In mystic states we both become one with the Absolute, and we become aware of our oneness. This is the everlasting and triumphant mystical tradition, hardly altered by differences of clime or creed. In Hinduism, in Neoplatonism, in Sufism, in Christian mysticism, in Whitmanism, we find the same recurring note, so that there is about mystical utterances an eternal unanimity which ought to make a critic stop and think, and which brings it about that the mystical classics have . . . neither birthday nor native land. Perpetually telling of the unity of man with God, their speech antedates languages, and they do not grow old!"—*Varieties of Religious Experience*, p. 419.

But he carries the doctrine further. Every day in the year, alike in the colleges of Benares and the villages of Mysore, men may be heard reciting this formula: *Ekam ęva advitîyam*—'One only without a second.' Such a formula, coming from a land of many gods, seems to Englishmen as surprising as it is beautiful. But what does it mean? 'One and no second'—god? No, that is not the way the Hindu fills up the ellipsis. 'One only and no second'—*anything*; and in that word he once more and decisively sets aside the universal testimony of our human consciousness. In the universe there is One—*no other*, *nothing else*; "there is no other seer but he, there is no other hearer but he;"[1] that is the burden of this high philosophy. It is the constant refrain of all its music; the theme, with infinite and most ingenious variations, of all its writings. Behind all, before all, in all, and beyond all is THE ONE. To this supreme and single entity the Hindu gives sometimes the name of Brahma,[2] and sometimes he calls it the Âtma,[3] *i.e.* the Self.

[1] *Bŗihadâraņyaka-Upanishad*, III. vii. 23.

[2] *Brahma*, the supreme soul of the universe, is a neuter noun, and is always to be carefully distinguished from Brahmâ (masculine), the first member of the Hindu triad. The root of the word is *Bŗih*, "to grow or increase," and its earliest significance, probably, was the expansive force of nature, spiritual and everywhere present, though everywhere unseen. Max Müller, in his *Hibbert Lectures* (p. 312), has suggested that "in choosing the neuter the ancient sages tried to express something that should be neither male nor female, that should be, in fact, as far removed from weak human nature as weak human language could well express it; something that should be higher than the masculine and feminine, not lower." Cf. Jacob's *Manual of Hindu Pantheism*, p. 2 (note).

[3] *Âtma* is used to signify both the spirit of the universe and the spirit of man, and its use in the philosophical literature of India is based on the idea that the principle of life which is in man is the same as that which animates nature. In its earliest occurrence Âtma means nothing more than

What, then, is Brahma? The sages falter here. He is said to be imperceptible to human vision, indescribable by human speech, absolutely inaccessible to human thought. "The eye goes not thither, nor speech, nor mind." A certain king, Vâshkali, asked a sage to explain Brahma, but he remained silent. The king repeated his command once and again, until at last the sage gave answer—"I tell it you but you do not understand; *s'ânto 'yam âtmâ*, this Self is silence!" If indeed speech is necessary, then all description must be by negatives. He is said to be unconditioned. That is a necessity, for if he be conditioned there must be somewhere something that conditions him—in which case unity has ended and duality begun. Qualify him and you limit him. I use the term "tree," a universal term for a given object; but speak of a "large" tree and you instantly limit the word by separating from it all trees that are not large; call it a "crooked" tree and you at once create schism in the species by cutting off all trees that are straight.[1] But it is essential to the Sole Reality that there shall be nothing like it, nothing different from it, and that within itself there shall be no variety. If there be anything with which to compare it, anything

"breath" in man and "wind" in the universe. But in the later Vedic literature Âtma attains a high degree of abstraction, and is said to be universally pervasive. It is used interchangeably with Brahma. When in common speech it is necessary to make a distinction, Brahma is spoken of as *Paramâtma*, the Supreme Self, and the individual is the *Jîvâtma*, the psychical principle in man. Cf. Macdonell's *Sanskrit Literature*, p. 218, and Barth's *Religions of India*, p. 71.

[1] "It is neither coarse nor fine; neither short nor long; neither red like fire, nor fluid like water; it is without shadow, without darkness, without air, without attachment, without taste, without smell, without eyes, without ears, without speech, without mind, without breath, without a mouth, without measure, having no within and no without." This account of Brahma occurs in the *Bṛihadâraṇyaka-Upanishad*, III. viii. 8.

with which to contrast it, or if it be itself divisible into parts, unity is destroyed and duality has begun.

There is one word which is continually recurrent in the writings that contain this philosophy. Whatever you may say of the Brahma, however describe him, the answer is *Nêti! nêti!* "not so, not so." Do you speak of him as subject? *Nêti! nêti!* for you thereby differentiate him from an object. Do you call him infinite? *Nêti! nêti!* for you start forthwith the image of the finite. He is not an empty abstraction, but he has no concrete. He is a necessity of thought, but beyond all comprehension. He is the impalpable and the immutable; the unbeginning and the unending; who neither apprehends nor may be apprehended; the unthinkable, the unspeakable; selfless, timeless, spaceless, causeless; the sole entity, the final reality. Beside him *there is no other, nothing else.*[1] That

[1] There is a famous passage in the *Bṛihadâraṇyaka-Upanishad* in which Yâjnavalkya says:—"When there is as it were duality, then one sees the other, one smells the other, one tastes the other, one salutes the other, one hears the other, one perceives the other, one touches the other, one knows the other; but when the Self only is all this, how should he see another, how should he smell another, how should he taste another, how should he salute another, how should he hear another, how should he touch another, how should he know another? How should he know Him by whom he knows all this? That Self is to be described by No, no! He is incomprehensible, for he cannot be comprehended; he is imperishable, for he cannot perish; he is unattached, for he does not attach himself; unfettered, he does not suffer, he does not fail. How should he know the knower?" IV. v. 15. Compare with this the description, by negatives, which is given of the Absolute by "the fountain-head of Christian mysticism," Dionysius the Areopagite. "The cause of all things is neither soul nor intellect . . . neither number, nor order, nor magnitude, nor littleness . . . neither essence, nor eternity, nor time," etc. etc. These qualifications Dionysius denies, "not because the truth falls short of them, but because it so infinitely excels them. . . . It is *super*-lucent, *super*-splendid, *super*-essential, . . . *super*-everything that can be named."—James' *Varieties of Religious Experience*, pp. 416, 417.

is the Everest of Indian philosophy, and most readers will feel that on that peak the air is so rarefied that it is almost impossible for common lungs to breathe it. Still we must pause here for a moment and try to take our bearings.

To discover the Infinite Unity in the finite diversity has been the untiring effort of sages in all lands and at all times. "The idea of God . . . meaning by that . . . the idea of an absolute principle of unity which binds 'all thinking things, all objects of all thought,' which is at once the source of being to all things that are, and of knowing to all things that know, . . . is the ultimate essential principle of our intelligence."[1] In other words, nothing can be truly known about anything until we know that to which everything else is essentially related; until we have found, so to speak, "the geometrical point through which pass all the threads which make up the web of possible experience."[2] Without some such principle of unity the universe would lack coherence, and science would then have lost its motive. Human conduct, too, would be for ever tentative, for in a world of isolated and uncontrolled elements the experience of to-day could yield no laws on which we might calculate with assurance to-morrow. Without an ultimate unity, reason would falter in permanent uncertainty, and religion would have neither starting-point nor goal.

Now this Unity the Vedântist philosophers find in Brahma. But what is Brahma? As we have seen, their

[1] E. Caird's *The Evolution of Religion*, vol. i. p. 68.

[2] Balfour's *Foundations of Belief*, p. 143.

description of Him, or more truly of It, is by negatives. By an exhaustive process of elimination they get rid of every conceivable quality and relation, and when they have stripped the entity bare, so that no single rag is left to help identification, they cry—"Behold, the One!" Let us hear them speak of this Sole Unity. It is *nir, nir, nir*, *i.e.* "destitute of." Brahma is *nir-guṇa* (without qualities), *nir-âkâra* (without form), *nir-vis'eṣ'a* (without difference), *nir-upâdhika* (without limitations). Now if in regard to a thing you deny its possession of any attribute and repudiate the possibility of any relation, what is left but bare existence? But bare existence—subject that knows no object and can therefore have no experience—is, if not a nonentity, at least an absolute vacuity.

Perhaps with a view to modify the harshness of such an inference, the *Vedânta-sâra*[1] describes "the Self" (*âtman*), which is a term used interchangeably with "Brahma," as *sac'c'idânanda*, or being, thought, and joy. It is *sat* = existence, τὸ ὄν, the real, the true. Now, in designating the Self as the real (*sat*), every other existence that can be either mentioned or imagined is thereby classed as the unreal (*asat*). But this lands us in a very singular position. The Hindu affirms a Sole Reality which makes of the mind that apprehends it and the tongue that proclaims it an unreality, so that that which is not reveals that which is, and the False unveils the True. The first word, then, in the above compound simply ascribes to Brahma pure being, and by implication denies existence to everything and everybody else.

[1] The *Vedânta-sâra* is a later epitome of the Vedânta doctrine, but it is everywhere accepted as authoritative.

It might be expected that the next two epithets would invest the first with something that redeems it from complete irrationality. Brahma, we are told, is *chit* = intelligence, and this finds authority in the Taittirîya Upanishad, where we read, "Self is knowledge." Is not this positive? But we must not be misled. The Self does not know, for then were there objects to be known; it is not even self-conscious, for then would it distinguish itself from something other than itself. In both cases unity would be at an end and duality would have begun. Moreover, as S'ankara says—"If it were a knowing subject, it would be limited by its objects and cognitions." In what sense, then, can *chit* be ascribed to Brahma? Not as predicating its attribute, but only as constituting its substance. Brahma is not a thinking being, but thought itself.[1] It is just a self-luminous entity; the source of light, like the sun, but within itself unilluminated; the source of intelligence, but knowing nothing—"for there is nothing second to that, other than that, apart from that, that it should know."[2]

Finally, Brahma is described as *ânanda* = bliss. But this again is purely negative. If it has no consciousness, it can, of course, know nothing about which to be happy, neither can it realise that it *is* happy. Brahma's bliss is said to be that of dreamless sleep. In such a sleep circumstance and condition are forgotten; pain, care, desire, and misery of every kind have ceased to be; and life persists in absolutely unruffled repose. But such bliss is merely the absence of everything that could in any degree

[1] Cf. *Vedânta-Sûtras*, in *S. B. E.*, p. xxv.

[2] *Bṛihadâraṇyaka-Upanishad.*

produce its opposite. Clearly, then, in all this we have reached no positive conception beyond this, that Brahma IS—simple, indiscrete, unrelated being.

Now, as we have seen, this affirmation of the sole existence of Brahma dismisses everything else into the limbo of unrealities. It is, to use a word of Hegel's, pure unrelieved *akosmism.* The Vedântic philosophy does not, like the Idealist philosophies of the West, acknowledge differences in the universe and seek a principle which will harmonise them; it simply denies the differences, and in that denial buries them. What it sets up, therefore, is not a unity at all—a reconciliation, that is, of opposing elements; it is an absolute, self-identic *unit*—"one only, without a second." But a bare unit, wholly self-contained and entirely unrelated, is impossible to human thought. For thought is essentially a unity in difference. "If the figures on your canvas are indistinguishable from the background, there is surely no picture to be seen. Some element of unlikeness, some germ of antagonism, some chance for discrimination, is essential to every act of knowing."[1] Take any idea that you will and it is seen at once to be composite. There can be no idea of pleasure which has not as its counterpart the idea of pain, or of bitter which has not as its counterpart the idea of sweet. Similarly the idea of mind always involves that of matter, and the infinite must ever presuppose the finite. We cannot think anything whatever except as contrasted with something else, and every act of the understanding is first of all the recognition of opposites—myself, the thinker, and that of which

[1] Fiske's *Through Nature to God*, p. 34.

I think—and then their reconciliation in a final unity. Eliminate any one of these elements, and the thought ceases. But this is just what the Vedântist tries to do. He affirms the One and denies all difference; but by a fatal irony the formula in which he does this illustrates the very difference that he denies. This has been so well demonstrated by a writer now in India, that I will quote his words in full.[1] "*Tat twam asi.* Here we have Subject, Object, and Relation in a sentence which is declared to be the highest pronouncement of philosophy on the universe. The Vedântin seeks by grammatical and rhetorical devices to reduce the *Tat* and the *Twam* to one and the same thing; if he could succeed, the saying would cease to be a thought. In the equation $x = x$, there is a difference no less than an identity. The equation means 'x on THIS side' is the same as 'x on THAT side'; or 'x which I think of NOW' is the same as 'x which I thought of THEN.' Destroy the differentiating attributes of x and you have destroyed the equation. If, as philosophers say, there is no absolute difference—that is, no entire separation between objects, for they must have at least a common relation in thought—so there is no absolute identity, for no identity can be so complete that there is not in it some differentiation of thought. To know absolute or Vedântic unity *we must cease to think.* If the Vedântist solution of the world-problem be correct, we can neither know that Absolute One while compassed with mind nor seek after it. Agnosticism, as prohibitive of action in relation to Brahma as it is of thought, must be ours."

The Vedântic doctrine of God is thus seen to be the

[1] *The Teaching of Swâmi Vivêkânanda,* by E. W. Thompson.

doctrine of the Unknowable in its baldest and most uncompromising form.[1] What that involves we shall have to consider at a later stage; but here it must be asked —Is there really anything to know? If Brahma were postulated as the universal which gathers up everything into itself and explains it, then indeed there *were* something to know; but it is not so, for the particular is denied at the very moment the universal is affirmed. With unflinching thoroughness the philosophers of India have divested Brahma of all relationship—and thereby robbed it of all content; for unrelatedness and emptiness are practically synonymous terms. Every positive possession, on whatever plane of life, demands and somewhere discovers correspondences for itself, and the number, subtlety, and complexity of such correspondences is a true criterion of the scale of being which has been reached. On the human plane the greatest man among us is always he who touches life at most points—who has, that is, the most varied gifts, alike spiritual and physical, intellectual and sympathetic. Conversely, the cutting down of correspondences means the proportionate shrinkage of being towards unimportance and disesteem. When,

[1] In this matter S'ankara of the eighth century and Mr. Herbert Spencer of the nineteenth, the sage of the East and the sage of the West, though so widely sundered, seem almost to join hands. S'ankara, echoing the language of the Upanishads, replies to every affirmation concerning Brahma —"Not that, not that." Mr. Spencer, speaking of the necessity in men to give shape to that Ultimate Existence which forms the basis of our intelligence," says—"We shall not err in doing this so long as we treat every notion we frame as merely a symbol, *utterly without resemblance to that for which it stands.*" He adds—"By continually seeking to know, and being continually thrown back with a deepened conviction of the impossibility of knowing, we may keep alive the consciousness that it is alike our highest wisdom and our highest duty to regard that through which all things exist as the Unknowable."—*First Principles*, p. 113.

therefore, the Vedântists, pursuing the path of abstraction, bring us to Brahma, the sole and unrelated, we can only reply—"A Being without relationships is, for us, a Being without content; and a Being without content can be of no help or interest to us. How such an Absolute can be known to exist at all, since it is unable to reveal itself through relationships, is a problem past solution. But even if its existence were certain, it must be such that the mind could offer it no regard and the heart no love. We yearn to find reality, complete and unalloyed, and you offer to us bare being; which is fundamental, indeed, but the very emptiest of all conceptions possible to the human mind. We search for the highest principle of thought, and you present to us blank unintelligence. We pray for light, and we are led into 'a night in which all cows look black.' We have asked for bread, and you have given us a stone; for a fish, and you have given us a serpent."

Why should men postulate this unintelligent and unintelligible Absolute? Why should they conjure up to themselves a vague impersonal One and offer That to us as Deity? Let us remind ourselves that this is a postulate made by persons. Personality is our distinction and the necessary starting-point of all our thought. It is that in which life finds its highest expression, and towards which it ever strives; and when we are seeking the highest, we are forced by the very constitution of our being to construe it in terms of personality. This seems to everybody but philosophers so obvious as to make the statement of it unnecessary. Most men are prepared to agree with Dr. Martineau when he says that "psychologically there can be no greater descent . . . than from the personal to the impersonal." Yet when we turn to the German metaphysician Deussen, who has expounded the Vedânta with a sympathy and fulness of knowledge beyond all praise, we find him saying—"Mark that the conception of God as a personal being . . . is merely exoteric, and does not give us an adequate knowledge of the Âtman;—and, indeed, when we consider what personality is, how narrow in its limitations, how closely connected with egoism, the counterpart of godly essence, who would think so low of God as to impute to Him personality?"[1] In this matter Mr. Herbert Spencer seems also to range himself with the Vedântists. It is true that he neither affirms nor denies personality of God; but nevertheless he decisively prefers to put aside personality and ascribe "something higher" to his Ultimate Cause. "Is it not just possible," he asks, "that there is a mode of being as much transcending Intelligence and Will, as these transcend mechanical motion?"[2] He frankly allows that we cannot conceive any such mode of being, but believing that the Ultimate must be greater in every respect than we can imagine, he condemns the attempt to assign to it any attributes whatsoever as derogatory and irreverent. But is the postulating of an impersonal Absolute anything other than a venture of despair? We are asked, by a stupendous act of faith, to take a leap from categories which we know to a category entirely different—a something of which we have no example and can form no conception. That something

[1] *Elements of Metaphysics*, p. 326. [2] *First Principles*, p. 109.

is to be regarded as the Ultimate Principle in the universe, though between the universe and it no similarity can be suggested and no relationship affirmed. But such a hiatus instantly destroys the coherence of things. *We* are in one realm and *that* is in another, and under the assumed conditions no thought of ours can ever truly mirror that. The late Professor Max Müller, notwithstanding all his admiration for the Vedânta, saw this clearly. He said—"This philosophy seems to solve all difficulties but one; and that is to find a natural approach to it from the position we occupy in looking at philosophical and religious problems."[1] Exactly; no "natural" approach ever can be found. We are bound by our constitution, and if the ultimate unity that we seek is not only infinitely higher in range, but also totally dissimilar in character and absolutely unrelated, then we may as well fling both science and philosophy to the winds, and content ourselves with growing pumpkins.

In the pursuit of knowledge it is fundamental that we should interpret things by means of the highest category within our reach. The very highest category known to modern philosophy is that of self-conscious intelligence or reason. If we must abandon this when we seek to go higher than man, why should we trust it when we look lower? But if, in that which is best in the life that we know, we may see a real manifestation, however faint and distant, of God; if in Him there are found in infinite degree and without any unworthy admixture those powers of Intelligence, Will, and Affection, which are the source of the greatest dignity and worth in ourselves,—then indeed

[1] *Râmakrishna*, p. 78.

the universe becomes homogeneous, and knowledge is made possible.

Wherein, to those who think with Vedântists, lies the difficulty of ascribing personality to God?

The primary difficulty lies here—that self-consciousness, which is of the very essence of personality, implies other consciousness and seems to create a duality. Such a conclusion is to a Vedântist the final condemnation of any postulate, and on the strength of it he repudiates the idea of personality in God. At every cost the ideal unity must be preserved. But, after all, what is unity? Is it simply an isolated point? Is it a bare enumeration? Is it a self-identic entity which within itself comprehends nothing, and without itself excludes nothing, and beside which nothing else is? In that case you cannot declare the Absolute Unity without self-contradiction, for, as Dr. Martineau has said in another connection, "in doing so you reserve your own personality as a thinking and assertive power," and while objectifying to yourselves the unity you destroy it. But it is possible and, if we are to think at all, necessary to use "unity" with a different meaning. Indeed, unity can only be properly known "as contradistinguished from plurality," and it "excludes what is diverse, so far only as that attempts to be anything by itself and to maintain isolation."[1] Perhaps it may be most truly defined as difference in solution, the harmony of oppositions. Now the strictest unity of which we have any experience is human personality, and it affords a

[1] F. H. Bradley, *Appearance and Reality*, pp. 224, 250.

complete demonstration of the point before us. For it is not a bare unit, having no variety within itself and no relationship to any difference outside itself. On the contrary, I cannot say "I am I" until the self as subject has, so to speak, stood apart from and thought about itself as object, thus at once creating and combining an internal variety; and this act of reflection is commonly forced upon me by something outside myself which is not me. "The true recognition of one's self as an 'I,'" says Lotze, "depends on the presence of a second point of reference to which the 'I' can oppose itself."[1] "I cannot think, or desire, or will without an object, which is either simply myself, or something associated with myself, or dissociated from myself considered as an object, in either case involving my objectivity to myself."[2] The diversity implied in personality is therefore fundamental and beyond all controversy. But the unity is no less clear. "However various and extended my objective world may become, it is still one object in relation to me; and however complex my relations to it, they are still my own, or one totality of relationship to that object."[3] Nature, *e.g.*, is not a mere casual appendix to mind, nor something lying around it in isolated and independent contiguity. It demands a subject, exists only for a subject, and is therefore in inseparable correlation with it. "Matter, as we know it, is always in synthesis with spirit,"[4] and that which does not exist in my thought does not for me as yet really exist at all. But however dissimilar in themselves the elements

[1] *The Philosophy of Religion* (Eng. trans.), p. 59.
[2] Illingworth, *Personality, Human and Divine*, p. 70.
[3] *Ibid.* p. 70. [4] *Ibid.* p. 47.

to which my mind accords place and hospitality, it at once relates, controls, and combines them in harmonious interplay; and out of Many makes an organic One. Nor does it accomplish this by any merely arbitrary effort of the imagination or will—an effort which it *might* decline to make, and to which any element *might* refuse to respond. It does it rather as the essential life pervading a great organism; the immanent unifying principle which finds therein its necessary and characteristic expression, and without which the organism would fall to pieces. In this case you cannot have the manifold except in and through the One.

But if human personality, properly understood, is an example of strict unity, why should the Vedântist, or any one else, in the interest of unity hesitate to ascribe personality to God? Postulate self-consciousness in Him, and He is then a subject who can become an object to Himself; but He is not thereby made two, for the elements, though distinct, are indivisible. Annihilate one, and you annihilate both. There is internal variety, but perfect unity. It is here that the Christian doctrine of the Trinity finds place. To many that doctrine has seemed an almost hopeless puzzle, and it may be allowed that the popular view of it, even yet, often ignores the One in confessing the Three. Nevertheless it has been rightly called "the most philosophical attempt to conceive of God as personal,"[1] and the Christian Fathers regarded it as the condition of rationally holding the unity of God.[2]

The doctrine stands as a decisive protest against any theory which regards God as impassive undifferentiated

[1] *Personality, Human and Divine*, p. 67. [2] *Lux Mundi*, p. 92.

Being, existing in isolation from all eternity, having no fellowships or relationships within Himself—a monad, which, being neither reason nor love, could be of no ultimate use to philosophy and no serious object of religion. It is therefore a direct protest against strict Vedântic teaching, and not less against every form of unitarian deism. It postulates in God not life merely, but the life of spirit, which is the highest that we can know. Now spirit is never in our experience a bare unit; it is always the home and bond of distinctions. It can express itself within itself; go forth from itself, and return to itself; it can think and will and love. But these functions of spirit involve relationships. If, then, God as spirit thinks, He is the eternal subject to whom must have been present an eternal object of contemplation. If God as spirit loves, then from all eternity He must have had an adequate object of love, and His nature must have comprised within itself the elements of a perfect fellowship. If God as spirit wills, then He must have found eternal expression for Himself. Thus the doctrine ascribes to God all that rich variety in perfect unity which is the distinction of personality. But personality in man is at best incomplete, unrealised, potential. "If, therefore, we are to think of God as personal, it must be by what is called the method of eminence (*via eminentiæ*)—the method, that is, which considers God as possessing, in transcendent perfection, the same attributes which are imperfectly possessed by man. He must, therefore, be pictured as One whose triunity has nothing potential or unrealised about it; whose triune elements are eternally actualised, by no outward influence, but from within; a Trinity in Unity; a social God, with all the conditions of personal existence internal to Himself." [1]

The doctrine of the Trinity speaks of "three persons in one God." It may well be that in treating of the immanent distinctions in the being of God, of "the Subject-objects of the Divine fellowship," language becomes halting and uncertain, and even misleading. The three "persons" are not separate individualities, but in "Father, Son, and Holy Spirit" we have figured forth to us the eternal relationships in which the One God realises and manifests Himself. "*The Father* is God as the source of all that is or can be: *the Son* is God as He exists to and for Himself, as He goes out from Himself in obedience to His nature of Perfect Love into the world, to create and spread abroad the Divine Life and Blessedness as this Sonship realised in finite beings; and as He realises that Sonship in human form, and returns to Himself in the Divine-human Christ: *the Holy Spirit* is God in His innermost being or essence, the principle of the life of both Father and Son; that in which God, both as Father and Son, does everything, and in which He comes to us and is in us increasingly through His manifestations." [2] Such a doctrine affirms at once the living unity of God and His immanence in the universe. He is one in Himself, and the whole world is in a real sense one in Him, being the outflow of His life and always sustained by it, the product of His love and Will, the constant object of His thought. No other doctrine can be named which guards unity—a true organic unity, and the only kind worthy to be considered—more jealously. Not

[1] *Personality, Human and Divine*, p. 74.

[2] W. L. Walker, *The Spirit and the Incarnation*, p. 337.

Vedântism, which is the most uncompromising form of Pantheism, for, as we shall see later, in order to secure Brahma's oneness and yet explain the world, it has to perpetrate a duality by inventing Mâyâ. Not Unitarianism, in any of its forms, since it banishes God into solitude, putting Him for ever out of living relation to the world, and leaving us with two inharmonious entities. The Christian doctrine maintains that which is dear to the Unitarian—the transcendence of God—without dissociating Him from His universe; and that which is dear to the European Pantheist—the immanence of God—without obliterating His personality; and that which is vital to the Vedântist—the real Unity—without denying the reality of God's world. The doctrine of the Personal Triune God stands as the sole sufficient safeguard of Unity.

There is one further difficulty, however, which will occur to many, both East and West, in regard to this matter. "*Is* the unity so completely assured in the doctrine of a personal God? It may well be that He is immanent in His universe, but how can that immanence be reconciled with the separate and distinct personality of Man?" Undoubtedly this question brings us face to face with a mystery, and seems to involve the limitation of God. The human spirit has individual will and responsibility; each is in a true sense one by itself; each may diverge from the other and from God in desire and determination; there is a certain "impenetrability" with which each one hedges itself round. But even so our spirits do not exist independently of His will. They derive their being from Him, are sustained by Him, and can at no point so break away from Him as to put their life outside

Himself. "Difficult as it may be to conceive, yet it is true that while God respects the personality He creates and the relationship He sets up, while He makes each man the possessor, within limits, of that responsible power of choice and will by which alone he becomes man, yet the whole of this creaturely personal existence never becomes an external fact to which God merely accommodates Himself. It remains an issue of His own life, while, notwithstanding, it is endowed with a personal independence (to use a somewhat unsuitable word) which He steadfastly maintains."[1] Thus, whatever limitation is implied in the existence of other personalities is the self-limitation of God, exercised in accordance with His own nature and character.[2]

This doctrine of a Triune Personal God is that which Christianity opposes to the "One-without-a-second" of Vedântism. Mere being, as Hegel says, is nothing at all. For God nothing less than Perfect Being can suffice, and perfect being carries with it a perfect mind and a perfect heart — Infinite Reason and Infinite Love. To the Vedântist God is the essence of life, but does not Himself live; He is the principle of intelligence, but does not know Himself; He is the sum of bliss, but cannot rejoice. Compare this with the Christian view of God: God is Spirit—therefore Intelligence and Will; God is Light—therefore holy and righteous; God is Love—therefore self-imparting. And He is these, not potentially, as is the case with us, but actually; not approximately, but perfectly.

His love is as great as His power,
And neither knows measure nor end.

[1] J. Scott Lidgett, *The Fatherhood of God*, p. 297.
[2] Cf. *Contentio Veritatis*, p. 37.

NOTE

The Hindu Triad

It will not be supposed by readers that there is any parallel between the Christian Trinity and the Hindu Trimûrti. The difference involved in the two conceptions has been so well stated by Dr. Fairbairn in his *Christ and Modern Theology*, that it will suffice here to quote his statement. He says :—

"The Hindu Trimûrti only represents the adaptation of a Pantheistic idea to historical conditions. The co-ordination of Brahma, Vishnu, and Siva is recent, and may be described as the result of a religious diplomacy, all the more real that it was unconscious and undesigned, and a metaphysical speculation that acted here just as it had acted everywhere. Each of the deities had a prior and very ancient history. They run back into the Vedic period, and are the survivals of different mythological schools and tendencies. Brahmâ (masculine) is the deification of the priestly idea, especially the act and efficacy of prayer ; Vishnu is a form of the sun-god, who as Sûrya or Savitri moved like a beneficent and radiant spirit across the face of the sky ; and Siva is the survivor of the ancient storm-gods, who swept from their homes in the Himâlayas with destructive force down upon the plains. These do not represent one religion, but distinct religions, or rather many different religions, each with its own customs, festivals, modes and objects of worship, and even geographical distribution. Then the Brahmă (neuter) in whom they are co-ordinated is the universal substance or soul ; of him or it all phenomenal being is a manifestation. He is no conscious reason, no home of ethical relations and distinctions, but only the ultimate essence or basis of all things. Every god and every man and every creature is in him as much as the sacred triad, and in all he appears or becomes incarnate. In other words, the system is a polytheistic and mythological Pantheism. But the Christian idea is the opposite of all this. God is personal, conscious, ethical ; the Godhead expresses this personal, conscious, and ethical being as immanent and essential. Man cannot be absorbed into God, or God individualised and distributed in man. The Persons in the Godhead are incapable of absorption into more abstract forms of being ; they represent God, not as an ever unfolding and enfolding substance, but as a necessary and eternal communion, the home of life and love."

SECTION III

THE ILLUSORY MANY

We are such stuff
As dreams are made of.—SHAKESPEARE.

Are we then driven to the conclusion that the external world is but a phantasm, the illusory assumption of common thought?—DR. JOHN CAIRD.

WE have lingered for some time on this topmost summit of Indian thought, and it is time now to descend. Here on these lower slopes, when we begin to recollect ourselves, we say—"Brahma the Sole Reality? But what, then, are we? And these that we see around—numberless creatures that are not identical with one another, nor with Brahma—what are these? Are they not real? If not, what are they, and whence come they? Explain them to us." That was the problem that presented itself to S'ankara and those that thought with him. This world of phenomena, how came it? Was it by Creation, or Emanation, or how?

"Not," said the Vedântist, "by creation"—and that for many reasons. How *could* it? Brahma is simple being; what, then, should have moved it to create? It could not be desire springing up within, for then were Brahma a differentiated being; nor yet appeal coming from without, for there was nothing without to appeal, and nothing within to be appealed to. How *could* it? Brahma is impersonal and without self-determination, while creation is an act of Personal Will. How *could* it? Brahma is unrelated—timeless, spaceless, causeless; but creation is a process which brings the Creator within the category of time. On all these grounds, and on others that might be named, creation as the explanation of phenomena was ruled out of court. Nothing else was possible when Brahma had once been postulated, for, as Dr. Fairbairn has rightly said, "out of an abstract of thought we cannot evolve the concrete of experience; for the very terms that define and express our ultimate abstraction take from it the power or faculty of creative movement."[1]

But if creation is inadmissible as an explanation of the universe, may we explain it by emanation? This seems to have been the doctrine of the Upanishads. To quote only two out of very many texts of similar import, we read—"As the spider comes out with its thread, or as small sparks come forth from fire, thus do all senses, all worlds, all Dévas, all beings come forth from that Self";[2] and again—"As the spider sends forth and draws in its thread, as plants grow on the earth, as from every man hairs spring forth on the head and the body, thus does everything arise here from the Indestructible."[3] In accordance with these passages, S'ankara defines Brahma as "that from which proceed the origination, sustentation, and retractation of this world,"[4] and he proceeds to explain that by this definition he intends to set forth Brahma

[1] *Christ in Modern Theology*, p. 409.
[2] *Bṛihadâraṇyaka-Upanishad*, II. i. 20.
[3] *Muṇḍaka-Upanishad*, I. i. 7.
[4] *Vedânta-Sûtras*, p. 283.

both as the material cause (*upâdâna kâraṇa*) of the world and as its operative cause. That Brahma is the operative cause, S'ankara says, "we have to conclude from the circumstance that there is no other guiding being," and with that he is satisfied. But on Brahma as material cause he dwells at large, calling up numerous illustrations from the Upanishads, which are naturally the stock-in-trade of every Vedântist to-day. What clay is to the earthen jar, or gold to the ring, or the sea to the foam, or the spider to the web, that is Brahma to the world—its substantial cause. But at this point we must remind ourselves that *in every cause must lie infolded that which is manifested in the effect.* Now, on the Vedânta theory, phenomena, if there be phenomena, can have only one cause. If, then, in the phenomena we see manifoldness and change, as we do, there seems no escape from the conclusion that they must exist also, in germ at least, in the Sole Cause, and that Brahma is not homogeneous, neither immutable, nor yet, since it has evolved relations, absolute. Postulate either creation or emanation, both of which involve physical change and a temporal process, and at one fell blow Brahma, the sole and changeless, is destroyed. "For the changeless Brahma cannot be the substratum of varying attributes."[1]

This objection was strongly pressed upon S'ankara, as indeed it must be pressed still. Looking around, men pointed to this tree and that star, to this dolt and that philosopher, and cried—"Brahma has in itself elements of manifoldness. As the tree has many branches, so Brahma possesses many powers and energies dependent on those

[1] *Vedânta-Sûtras*, p. 327.

powers. Unity and manifoldness must therefore both be true. Thus, a tree considered in itself is one, but it is manifold if viewed as having branches; so the sea in itself is one, but manifold as having waves and foam; so the clay in itself is one, but manifold if viewed with regard to the jars and dishes made of it."[1] S'ankara's reply to this common-sense objection is in his most characteristic style. He first of all quotes a famous passage from the *Chhândogya Upanishad*, in which Aruni seeks to teach to his son S'vetaketu that, knowing which, all else is known. "My dear," says the father, "as by one clod of clay all that is made of clay is known, the difference (*vikâra*)[2] being only a name arising from speech, but the truth being that all is clay; and as, my dear, by one nugget of gold all that is made of gold is known, the difference being only a name arising from speech, but the truth being that all is gold; and as, my dear, by one pair of nail scissors all that is made of iron is known, the difference being only a name arising from speech, but the truth being that all is iron,—thus, my dear, is that instruction." On this S'ankara remarks —"These modifications or effects (such as jars, dishes, pails, etc.) are names only, exist through or originate from speech only, while in reality there exists no such thing as a modification. In so far as they are names (individual effects distinguished by names) they are untrue; in so far as they are clay, they are true."[3] By this he means that *the Cause only is true*, while the effects are false; that "the many as many has only a nominal existence, reality

[1] *Vedânta-Sûtras*, pp. 321, 322.
[2] *Vikâra*=difference, variety, change by form and name.
[3] *Vedânta-Sûtras*, p. 320.

residing in the one."[1] Herein lies the difference between the Pantheism of India and the Pantheism of the West. According to the teaching of the West, God is the sum or totality of phenomena, while according to the Vedânta God is the one underlying essence of phenomena, which are but the results of *name and form* (*nâma, rûpa*) superimposed upon the essence.[2] Emerson, in his most attractive poem, makes Brahma say—

> They reckon ill who leave me out;
> When me they fly, I am the wings;
> I am the doubter and the doubt,
> And I the hymn the Brâhman sings.

But in that verse he represents the Pantheism of the West rather than that of India. The Vedântist would say—"There are no wings, no doubter or doubts, neither any Brâhman; these are name and form merely, and nothing really is but the 'I,' Brahma."

So the Vedântist denies both creation and emanation, and says that all things are *Illusion*. "The entire universe, movable and immovable, comprising bodies, intellects, and the organs, everything that is seen or heard, from Brahmâ[3] down to a tuft of grass . . . is that which is known as Illusion."[4] But what is Illusion? The Hindu distinguishes three kinds of existence. There is true existence, the really real (*pâramârthika*), which is Brahma. There is false existence (*mithyâ*), existence merely in

[1] Gough's *Philosophy of the Upanishads*, p. 250.

[2] See quotation from *Brahmavâdin* in Slater's *Higher Hinduism*, p. 88.

[3] Brahmâ (masculine) must be distinguished from Brahma (neuter). The latter is the impersonal Self, the Ultimate One. But Brahmâ is the illusory personal God and the first member of the Hindu Triad.

[4] Quoted by Jacob from *Adhyâtma-Râmâyaṇa*.

conception, as when we speak of a round square, or the son of a childless woman: impossible actually, but possible to thought. And finally, there is illusory, phenomenal existence (*vyâvahârika*), which differs from false existence in this—that though it is in itself unreal, *it has something real behind it.* It is illustrated by the case of the man who, seeing a rope at dusk, mistakes it for a snake, or seeing mother-of-pearl, supposes it to be silver. He does not see what he thinks he sees; that is his illusion. But the illusion is not wholly baseless. He would not imagine the snake if there were no rope, or the silver if there were no mother-of-pearl. So behind the phenomena which we mistakenly suppose that we see, there is an eternal reality. Nevertheless, what we see is not what we think, is indeed nothing at all; and this doctrine the Vedântist preaches with untiring persistence and with great variety of illustration. Passing through the Suez Canal, you look across the desert—dry, treeless, unpromising. Then suddenly you behold lakes and ships and trees, a picture of life, fertility, and beauty, where all had been waste and dead. It is the mirage—real enough to your perception, though it vanishes when you approach it. "That," says the Vedântist, "is what you and I are, and all the world beside—as vivid and interesting as a mirage, and as unsubstantial." That is illusory existence. Or, take another of their stock illustrations. You dream, and in your dream suppose yourself another; you receive his honours, sob over his griefs, live his life—and then awaken to find you are not him, but you. Yet how real and impressive and undeniable it all was while it lasted! It was an illusory existence. And such we are told is our life—real enough from the standpoint of daily experience; but from the standpoint of metaphysical knowledge a wild hallucination, a tyrannous fiction.

Now, limiting ourselves for the moment to these illustrations, we have to ask—*Who* saw the mirage? *Who* dreams the dream? The answer we know already. The being that dreams and that mistakenly perceives is Brahma. But how can Brahma—the inert, impassive, impersonal—dream, and why should it? These are crucial questions, and we cannot of ourselves answer them. We can only set down what the Hindu sages have said. They tell us that the principle of reality (Brahma) has been everlastingly associated with "an inexplicable principle of unreality," to which they give the name of Mâyâ. "It is from the fictitious union of these principles, the one real, the other only a self-feigned fiction, that the spheres and the migrating forms of life, the external and internal world, proceed."[1]

In treating of Mâyâ,[2] therefore, we are really dealing with the Vedântist's view of cosmogony.

To describe Mâyâ is well-nigh an impossibility. S'ankara, following earlier writers, tells us we must not call it real (*sat*), but neither may we call it unreal (*asat*). It must not be called real, for that were to depose Brahma as the Sole Reality. Yet we may not say that it is quite unreal, since it produces the appearance of the world which *seems* so real. But this is only to confess that nobody knows anything about it, except that it is a desperate

[1] *Philosophy of the Upanishads*, p. 47.

[2] Other names for Mâyâ are Avidyâ and Ajnâna, both of which mean Nescience or Ignorance.

supposition adopted to relieve the old philosophers of India in their struggle to maintain an ideal unity. It is far easier to indicate the function which Mâyâ serves than to describe its nature. Technically it is called an *upâdhi* —that which is "put down near" a thing and makes it appear something other than it is; as when a red rose is put down near a white crystal and makes the crystal appear red.[1] Mâyâ, then, is that which conditions the unconditioned Brahma. It is credited with two powers: it envelops or conceals (*âvaraṇa*) and projects (*vikshépa*). That is to say, this strange principle first of all hides Brahma from itself, veils to it its true nature, as a cloud might veil the sun, so that it becomes capable of the conceit of personality; and then it leads Brahma, as a method of realising its illusory personality, to project "the phantasmagoria of a world." Or, to revert to the figure of a moment ago, Mâyâ sets Brahma *dreaming* that it is something and somebody quite other than itself. Herein lies the whole story, according to the Vedântist, of this phenomenal universe. Truly the power of Mâyâ must be miraculous! The real eternal Brahma is, as we have seen, figured as in dreamless sleep—without thought, without desire, without will. But directly Mâyâ casts its spell over Brahma, there is a change in the essentially unchangeable; the dreamless one dreams, and in that dream plans, desires, and creates, like one endowed with complete personality.

It will be seen at once that Brahma *plus* Mâyâ differs essentially from the Brahma of which hitherto we have been thinking and writing. That was the Ultimate

[1] Cf. *Hindu Pantheism*, p. 59.

Principle, timeless, spaceless, causeless, inaccessible to thought and impossible of description; but Brahma, wrought upon and, we might almost say, hoodwinked by Mâyâ, becomes a personal God—a being, therefore, and not merely a principle; one who can know and be known, love and be loved. To this personalised being, thus illusorily developed, the Vedântists give the name *Îs'vara;* and in this way they have obtained for themselves what they were by no means able to do without—a God to whom they could direct their worship. Yet how extraordinary the position to which they managed to bring themselves. The only path by which the Divine Being might attain self-knowledge was, in the opinion of these philosophers, self-deception![1]

Îs'vara, then, *the personal God of Vedântism, is the first and supreme product of Illusion* (Brahma+Mâyâ), and it is from him that all the manifold of experience which we call phenomena springs. He is depicted as the great magician[2] who, with inexhaustible cunning and wholly for his own amusement, produces an endless variety of effects. But all that he produces is appearance only, sheer sleight-of-hand on an infinite scale, and destitute of all ordered and reliable

[1] Cf. Slater's *Higher Hinduism*, p. 96.

[2] See *Vedânta-Sûtras*, II. i. 33. The text runs: "Brahma's creative activity is mere sport such as we see in ordinary life." S'ankara thus comments on the passage—"We see in everyday life that certain doings of princes, or other men of high position who have no unfulfilled desires left, have no reference to any extraneous purpose, but proceed from mere sportfulness, as for instance their recreations in places of amusement. We further see that the process of inhalation and exhalation is going on without reference to any extraneous purpose, merely following the law of its own nature. Analogously, the activity of the Lord also may be supposed to be mere sport, proceeding from its own nature, without reference to any purpose."

sequence. He has no motive outside himself for his activity. There *is* nothing that is not himself, the freak of his mood, the shadow of his substance, the projection of his being. He is stage and actor, play and audience, all in one. This illusory God is not to be separated in thought from any part of his illusory creation. He is

> The lord of all, himself through all diffused.

If *any* difference between himself and his creation be permissible, even to the contemplation of a moment, it may only be figured as the difference between the wave and the sea, or between the sparkle in the dewdrop and the sun, which to the Vedântist is not more than a difference in name and form.

It is thus that we come upon the great idea of the omnipenetrativeness of God. The world, whatever it is, real or mere semblance, is not something outside God. Whatever He is, illusory Creator or eternal essence, He is within and through it all, the Power which first projects and then permeates the whole. This is the witness which Pantheistic India has all along borne to the world. However erratic his exposition, however grotesque his illustration, every Vedântist will cry—

> Earth's crammed with heaven,
> And every common bush afire with God.

The idea is constantly recurrent in the ancient books of India. In one of the Upanishads, for instance, we find these words:—"He who dwells in the mind, . . . whom the mind does not know, whose body the mind is, and who rules the mind within, he is thy Self, the ruler within, the immortal."[1] There are three pages like this, dealing with eye, ear, tongue, skin, sun, moon, stars, air, fire, water, etc., and closing with this—the essential dogma of Vedântism—"There is no other seer but he, there is no other hearer but he, there is no other knower but he." But the most elaborate expression of God's immanence, perhaps, is to be found in the *Bhagavad Gîta*—"Of weapons of war I am the thunderbolt . . . of purifiers I am the wind . . . of creations I am the beginning and the end, and I am also the middle. . . . I am Eternal Time. . . . I am Death that seizes all, and the Source of all that are to come. . . . I am Fame, Fortune, and Speech, Memory, Intelligence, Constancy, Patience. . . . I am the Dice-play of the fraudulent, and the Splendour of the splendid. . . . Of things that subdue I am the Rod, and the Polity of those who seek to conquer. Of secret things I am Silence, and the Knowledge of those who know."[2]

> Living or lifeless, still or stirred, whatever beings be,
> None of them is in all the worlds, but it exists by Me!

Îs′vara, in his character as magician, is credited with the creation of many things—gods and solid worlds and transmigrating sentiencies; but it will be enough for us to inquire here what in all this scheme of things we ourselves are. To that the Vedântist's answer cannot be doubtful. We are simply one trick of the mighty conjuror, the illusory output of his wondrous cunning. If this judgment had reference only to our physical frame, many would hear it without serious demur. It is external,

[1] *Brihadâranyaka-Upanishad*, III. vii. 21–23 (*S. B. E.*).
[2] *Bhagavad Gîta*, x. 20–39. Translated by Davies.

transient, one of the passing shows of things. But what about the Ego which is encaged within the body? Is that illusory also? "Yes," says the Vedântist psychologist; "perception, memory, will, conscience—these are not *me.* Perception is merely a window through which my self looks out; memory, a door through which my self looks back; will, an instrument of which my self makes use. These and such like faculties simply constitute the 'subtle' body enclosing the self. That body lasts longer than this gross outer body, and accompanies me in all my transmigrations; but it, too, is physical, that is, illusory, and must disappear like the mirage." Those readers who have been in Egypt will have been struck with the way in which some of the women there enswathe themselves in fold after fold of linen, so that they look like so many peripatetic packages of cloth. But travellers know, of course, that the woman herself in every case is something quite other than that which they see. So the self, hidden away by folds of gross flesh, which we call body, and by other folds of subtle flesh, which we call mind, is something quite other than either, and is only related to them in imagination. The self within is the one and only Self, Brahma, enclosed within every illusory individual, *but one all the time*—"as one and the same face may be reflected in a succession of mirrors."

This doctrine is sufficiently astonishing, for it means nothing less than that the soul in every one of us must be the complete undivided Brahma; not a part, or a modification of the Eternal Self, but the very Brahma. Yet, however astonishing, this is a doctrine that S′ankara accepts and contends for. He will not allow that the individual soul is *part* of Brahma; because Brahma, not existing either in time or space, is of necessity indivisible (*akhaṇḍa*). Neither can he allow it to be a modification of Brahma, for that would presuppose an entity other than the One as bringing about the modification, and some change in the Self which is by its definition unchangeable. Thus, then, the great truth which every Vedântist desires to realise is this—that, stripped of all wrappings, disencumbered of all illusions, he is himself, wholly and without any sort of discount, the Everlasting One. The fact that he does not realise it at present is due to the fatal alliance between Brahma and Mâyâ, whereby Brahma is transformed into Îs′vara.

In considering this wonderful theory, it will be well, in the first place, that we should suggest those objections which appeal most immediately to the Hindu. At a later stage we may discuss the whole question from a more general point of view. To begin with, then, it is held by all Vedântists that the phenomenal world is an eternal process. Now, as that process is due to the association of Mâyâ with Brahma, it follows that there must be two entities, co-ordinate and eternal. "Plainly, then," we affirm, "unity has never existed, and duality has been the everlasting rule." "No," says the Hindu; "as the possibility of the future tree pre-exists in the seed of the tree, without the seed becoming any the less a one and only seed, so Brahma, though associated with Mâyâ, is not less the one and only being." It is curious how the Hindu, who affirms the unreal character of all phenomena, habitually uses these same phenomena to illustrate and prove his assertions about the Real. But these illustrations are often the Hindu's betrayal, and this is a case in point. Here is the seed—it is one undoubtedly, and, without destroying its unity, there exists within it the possibility of the tree. But that possibility will never become an actuality until something else, not the seed—soil and moisture and heat—have brought their influence to bear upon it. Brahma is the seed if you will, and from Brahma is to be developed the world of phenomena; but something else, as eternal as Brahma, must act upon it before the development takes place, and that something is Mâyâ. Judged by the people's own illustration, therefore, unity can never have existed.

But there arises, in the next place, a difficulty even still more serious. The Vedântists of necessity admit that Mâyâ is eternal (*anâdimâyâ*). Of necessity, we say, for if this were not admitted they would have to account for the first appearance of Mâyâ, the reason and the manner of it—which would be a task quite beyond even their utmost subtlety. Not only is Mâyâ postulated as eternal, however, but it is also affirmed to be *eternally associated with Brahma.* In that case it is inevitable that we should ask—Has there ever been a period at which Brahma was absolute and unconditioned? No being, not even an infinite one, could be both unconditioned and conditioned at the same time. To live in dreamless sleep, and at the same time to exercise all the activities of the waking state, is one of the fixed impossibilities. Vedântists, therefore, must take their choice. Either Brahma is the eternally unconditioned one, in which case they must start a new theory of phenomena, or else it is the eternally conditioned one, in which case the absolute Brahma, which has all along been their first and supreme postulate, never existed except as a figment of their own illusory brain.

Again, the question must be raised as to whether this theory of Mâyâ does not preclude all possibility of final salvation. We have shown in an earlier section of this volume that the Hindu hopes for ultimate release from the cycle of births and deaths, and expects, when once he realises that he is indeed the Brahma, to attain the bliss of dreamless sleep. But the fact that I am a transmigrating entity is, *ex hypothesi*, due to the action of Mâyâ upon Brahma. Does Mâyâ, then, ever cease to operate? Or can it be said that Mâyâ operates in part on Brahma and in part leaves it unaffected? And if the latter alternative be the true one, must we not suppose that as souls attain release an increasing portion of Brahma is being steadily reclaimed from Mâyâ's influence, so that conceivably Brahma will sometime be finally separated from that which conditions it? These questions are of the most crucial order, and plunge the Vedântist in difficulties from which he cannot possibly escape. If, as we have seen, each individual soul be the complete Brahma, then when *one* such soul escapes from the coil of temporal existence, Mâyâ and Brahma should become finally divorced, and phenomena should for ever cease. That conclusion seems irresistible. If, however, in face of the continuance of phenomena, this conclusion meets with demur, we must next assume that part of Brahma (represented by the souls that have attained final salvation) has escaped the thraldom of Mâyâ, while another part (represented by those of us who are yet on the wheel) still remains under the veil. But this is to divide the indivisible and to destroy Brahma.

Let that pass, however, and let us assume, with the Hindus, that all at last will penetrate the mists with which Mâyâ has enveloped them, and realise that they are one with the unconditioned Brahma. In that case we must necessarily arrive at a state of things in which these entities dwell finally apart, neither influencing or being influenced by the other. But not only does this involve the Vedântist in an unending duality, but it compels him to abandon the tenet of the eternity of the phenomenal process. Turn which way he will, he finds himself in trouble, and if he will not set aside the theory of Mâyâ he has no alternative but to relinquish the hope of final salvation.

SECTION IV

IDEALISM—EAST AND WEST

Suppose that the sun is shining on the sea, and that his light is broken by the waves into a multitude of lesser lights, of all colours and of all forms; and suppose that the sea is conscious of this multitude of lights, this diversity of shifting colours, this plurality of dancing forms, would this consciousness contain or represent the truth, the real? Certainly it would not. The objectively true, the real in itself, is in this case the sun in the heavens, the one permanent, the persistent in colour and form. Its diversified appearance in the sea, the dispersion of its light in myriad colours and in myriad forms, is nothing and represents nothing which substantially exists; but is only something which exists phenomenally, that is, unsubstantially and unreally, in the sea.—FERRIER'S *Illustration of the Teaching of Xenophanes*, quoted by GOUGH.

The heavens declare the glory of God; and the firmament sheweth His handywork.—PSALM xix. 1 (R.V.).

In Him were all things created, in the heavens and upon the earth, things visible and things invisible, whether thrones or dominions or principalities or powers; all things have been created through Him and unto Him; and He is before all things, and in Him all things consist.—ST. PAUL in Colossians, i. 16, 17 (R.V.).

THE considerations on which we have just been dwelling must seem almost hopelessly remote from the life and interest of the average English reader, though they are undoubtedly pertinent and vital to multitudes of people in India. But the doctrine of Mâyâ has aspects which are as congruous to the thought of the West as truly as to the thought of the East, and to these we now turn.

One of the great old commentators of India, Mâdhavâchârya, remarks very suggestively on "the diverse programme which the announcement of sunset would dictate to a dacoit, a debauchee, and a devotee." It is always so: out of the same thing different minds extract very different meanings. Nowhere, perhaps, is this more manifest than in the varying interpretations which men have given to natural phenomena. The world in which we live, the things we see around us—are these real? The table on which I write these words—is it a veritable, palpable table or merely an idea in my brain? Most men have their answer ready to such questions, and treat the questioners with scant courtesy, bidding them test their doubt by running their head against a post or putting their hand in the fire! But scorn does not kill philosophy, and in all thinking lands and at all times the doubt has found persistent expression. "Is the world a real world? If we and everybody else were away, would *it* be here all the same? If there were no eye to see and no mind to perceive, would the sun still shine, the flowers bloom and the dewdrops glisten? Is matter a self-sufficing independent existence, or are 'things' only the innate subjective perceptions of the intellect?" These questions have become vocal alike in East and West, and the various answers given have had a generic likeness, whether in Asia or in Europe. Some have allowed mind and matter equal and independent reality; others have allowed reality to matter only and entombed mind therein; others, again, have allowed mind only to be real, and have attributed to it the creation of matter; while a fourth class have repudiated mind and matter both, and have regarded the whole system of things as simply "a play of phantasms in a void." As some one has wittily put it, when one school cries—"No matter," a second retorts—"Never mind"; while a third caps both by rejoining—"Never mind and no matter."

These alternatives were debated as eagerly and patiently in the forest-schools of ancient India as they have been since in any of the learned societies of Europe. All views found voice there — those of Realist (*Sarvâstitva-vâdin*), Idealist (*Vijnânavâdin*), and Nihilist (*S'ûnya-vâdin*), just as in the West. What position did the Vedântists hold in these discussions? It is commonly assumed that they are to be classed as idealists—men who maintain that thought only is real. It has been suggested that the Vedântist is closely akin in his philosophical creed to our British Berkeley, and this suggestion has in recent years been dwelt upon by Hindus with much frequency and fervour of gratitude. The analogy between the two is, however, an extremely superficial one. Speaking broadly, both Berkeley and the Vedântists affirm that Spirit is the supreme reality in the universe; and both teach that "things" are merely phenomena, and apart from Spirit nothing at all. But directly we begin to probe these statements, the seeming similarity disappears in yawning differences that refuse to be bridged. The point that Berkeley emphasised was this: that "that alone exists which is perceived," and that all talk of the existence of "things" *apart from perception* is both baseless and dangerous. Matter as a separate entity, independent of mind or consciousness, he would not concede. Such concession, he maintained, could only land men in the quagmire of materialism, and against materialism he contended with all his might. He stood for the truth and reality of *spirit*—our own and the Eternal Spirit—and of *ideas.* "The former are active, indivisible substances; the latter are inert, fleeting, dependent beings, which subsist not by themselves, but are supported by, or exist, in minds or spiritual substances." He was thus the advocate of Mind as the paramount principle in the universe. But did not Berkeley in this way discredit the universe? Did he not impeach alike its reality and its worth by reducing it all to mere appearance? To read him thus is to misapprehend him completely. His own declaration on this point is explicit enough. He says—"In denying the things perceived by sense an existence independent of the substance or support wherein they may exist, we detract nothing from the received opinion of their *reality* . . . all the difference is that, according to us, the unthinking beings perceived by sense have no existence distinct from being perceived, and cannot therefore exist in any other substance than those unextended indivisible substances or *spirits* which act and think and perceive them; whereas philosophers vulgarly hold the sensible qualities do exist in an inert, extended, unperceiving substance which they call *matter*, to which they attribute a natural subsistence exterior to all thinking things, or distinct from being perceived by any mind whatsoever, even the eternal mind of the Creator."[1] Still more clearly, if possible, he says in the same *Treatise*—"I do not

[1] *Principles of Human Knowledge*, § 91.

argue against the existence of any one thing that we can apprehend either by sensation or reflection. That the changes I see with my eyes, and touch with my hands, do exist, really exist, I make not the least question. The only thing whose existence I deny is that which philosophers call mátter, or corporeal substance." The truth is that Berkeley regarded the physical universe with the most reverent and interested attention; he dwelt with special delight upon the steady phenomenal order which is everywhere apparent and which makes science possible; and he showed how through the medium of this phenomenal order a moral government with a moral purpose is being conducted. The most authoritative exponent of Berkeley, Dr. Campbell Fraser, tells us that his thought "becomes, when we pursue it further than he did, a sublime intuition of the phenomenal realities of sense, inorganic and organic, as established media for the intellectual education of finite spirits by means of physical sciences; for intercourse between individual moral agents; and for a revelation of the Eternal Spirit, in whom merely things of sense and moral agents too have their being." Thus to Berkeley God was real; the human spirit was real; and the external world, though not an independent material entity, had nevertheless perfect reality as the ordered impression of Divine ideas made upon the human spirit.

But this is diametrically opposed to the position of the Vedântists as expounded by S'ankara. It is true that on occasion S'ankara, who could be an opportunist in argument, maintains the validity of consciousness, and, like any robust realist, laughs at the man who would translate this solid earth and all the things around us into mere appearance. "Why should we pay attention," he says, "to the words of a man who, while conscious of an outward thing through its approximation to his senses, affirms that he is conscious of no outward thing, and that no such thing exists, any more than we listen to a man who, while he is eating and experiencing the feeling of satisfaction, avers that he does not eat and does not feel satisfied?"[1] This, however, is not the real S'ankara, and these words are not the words of a true Vedântist. He spoke there simply *as a psychologist* dealing with the undeniable facts of universal consciousness. But the Vedântist has, properly speaking, no business whatever with psychology; his whole concern is with ontology, for by the hypothesis there is nothing else for him to concern himself about. The consistent Vedântist cannot rightly admit any reality in phenomena, nor any truth in our perception of phenomena. To him perceiver *and* perceived are both alike an illusion. It is here that Berkeley and S'ankara part irreconcilably. Berkeley, while ascribing a phenomenal reality to the external world, maintained that finite mind was a reality of another order—capable of acting from itself and for itself, and thus having marks which cannot be found in mere phenomena. In truth he placed God and the finite spirit in precisely the same order of reality, and for the latter contended that in its own degree it was free, causal and responsible; an entity that was neither to be merged in phenomena nor yet extinguished in God. In this contention Berkeley drew himself for ever clear of Pantheism. No man who accepts the testimony of human consciousness, and believes in his

[1] *Vedânta-Sûtras*, II. ii. 28.

own real and separate personality, can ever be a true Pantheist; and on this point Berkeley spoke with clear decisiveness and manifest conviction. He was a genuine Theist.

But the main tenet of Vedântism—the very heart of it, without which it has no existence—is the sole reality of Brahma, and by consequence the total unreality and nothingness of everything else besides, whether nature or man. Doubtless this is stating the position with uncompromising bluntness, and present-day Hindus certainly seem to shy at such an expression of it. But no laboured subtleties of language can ever successfully hide the fact. S′ankara had no hesitation whatever in admitting it. This is his testimony—"The whole order of subject and object, of migrating souls and of their fruition of recompenses, is, apart from the Self, unreal; in like manner, as the ether in this and that pot or jar is nothing else than the ether at large, that permeates all things, itself one and undivided; and in like manner as the waters of a mirage are nothing else than the sands of the desert, seen for awhile and vanishing, and having no real existence." Semblance, optical illusion, mere differentiation of name and form without any differentiation of substance—this is how the universe is to be regarded. "The ocean is so much water, and the foam, the ripples, the waves, and the bubbles that arise out of that water, are alike one with it, and yet they differ among themselves. The foam is not the ripple, the ripple is not the wave, the wave is not the bubble; and yet the foam is water, the ripple is water, the wave is water, the bubble is water. . . . The soul is not the environment, the environment is not the soul; the soul is Self, the environment is Self." Nothing truly is but God.

i. We may at once acknowledge that in this doctrine the Hindu proclaims that it is the Unseen which is the Real, and thereby makes a useful and effective protest against materialism. He, at any rate, should never seek in the sensuous that satisfaction for the soul which can be found only in God. But in proclaiming the reality of the unseen he affirms also the unreality of the seen. It is hard to say which is the graver error—that which tethers the soul to the earth, or that which utterly discredits the earth and refuses to make it even a stepping-stone to heaven. At any rate, the malign influence of this doctrine is manifest enough in the life and work of the people of India. There has been among them a notorious disesteem for facts, an almost ostentatious disbelief in reality. Look at the literature which India has produced. It has been prolific in fable, but it has been barren in history; it has been overgrown with speculation, but it includes hardly any works of careful observation. Its great and ancient books expound to us an eccentric geography and a most romantic astronomy; but there are few records of even the smallest scientific value. If, again, we consider Indian art, we find depicted shapes such as never were "on sea or land"—forms wildly original, sometimes repulsive, and often ludicrously disproportioned; but there has seldom been any really careful attempt to reproduce the forms of nature or to exhibit with accuracy the best types of human beauty. This doctrine of Mâyâ has lain like a cankerworm at the root of the literature, art, and science of India. Nor can this be wondered at. The more convinced and thorough-going a man is in his Vedântism, the more profoundly must he distrust nature in all its forms. At the best he can only feel towards it as a prisoner feels towards the cell which hides from him the light and freedom of the life without. He cannot turn to it in any of its aspects and find therein hints and revelations of the Supreme One. Nature, if it is anything at all, is a mask that hides God, not a window that reveals Him. He cannot legitimately construe anything that he sees into an expression of the mind and character of God. No Vedântist could ever have written the nineteenth Psalm. To him "the heavens" do *not*, in any real sense, "declare the glory of God"; for "the heavens" are an illusion and God is unknowable. Nature has no true ministry for such a man—inspires no song, resolves no doubt, soothes no sorrow, and brings no revelation.

To the Christian, nature necessarily bears a very different interpretation. He may not dismiss it as unreal; he does not disdain it as misleading. He regards it as the true manifestation of Spirit, and reverences it as instinct with spiritual significance. For him the world is "one vast apocalypse of God," Who created it and ever sustains and animates it. St. Paul affirmed alike what is fundamental in Theism and what is fundamental in Pantheism when to the men of Athens he declared "the God that made the world and all things therein . . . Lord of heaven and earth"; and then added—"for in Him we live and move and have our being."[1] There we have transcendence; there, also, we have immanence.

[1] The Acts of the Apostles, xvii. 24, 28 (R.V.).

These are, in truth, the commonplaces of Bible teaching, though it has happened in the course of history that due emphasis has not been consistently laid on both. But the full Christian view of nature is only attained when we confess that "all things have been created through Him (Christ) and unto Him; and He is before all things, and in Him all things consist."[1]

Christ is at once the ground of creation and its goal. He is the ground of creation; for God, in order to create, must necessarily go out from Himself; the Absolute must enter into relation. But there is no going forth of the Father except in and through the Son, and therefore it is that we are told that "all things were made by Him, and without Him was not anything made that hath been made."[2]

Christ is, further, the goal of creation. It is towards the perfect realisation of Himself in His Son, and in those who should be "conformed to the image of His Son," that in nature God has been progressively working. Thus the universe in all stages of its history, and in all forms of its life, has been the outcome of the Father's will in Christ, and has been permeated and controlled by His holy and loving purpose. It is in this sense that the sacred writers have told us that "of Him, and through Him, and *unto* Him, are all things";[3] and that Christian poets have felt

A sense sublime
Of something far more deeply interfused,
Whose dwelling is the light of setting suns,
And the round ocean, and the living air,

[1] Col. i. 16, 17 (R.V.). [2] S. John i. 3 (R.V.).
[3] Romans xi. 36 (R.V.).

And the blue sky, and in the mind of man;
A motion and a spirit that impels
All thinking things, all objects of all thought,
And rolls through all things.

It is under the influence of sentiments like these that in Christian lands beyond all others there has been developed an æsthetic delight in scenery and a steady devotion to physical science. Not merely for utilitarian purposes have men interrogated the heavens and sought to disentomb the secrets of the earth. There has been also the desire and expectation that in nature they would find God's witness to Himself. The objection is frequently made that there are natural phenomena which, if God is good and working towards moral ends, contradict the idea of His immanent control. But the perplexity is substantially relieved if we remember that to the best of our knowledge God works on the plan of development, and that to some things, therefore, there still attaches the imperfection of the rudimentary stage. We must remember, further, that though all creatures are dependent on God, they are endowed with a relative independence—an independence which, in certain stages of being, makes it possible that there should be some deflection from the Divine will and purpose. Such deflection is bound to issue in that which is incongruous and disastrous. "Incomplete or perverted development" will explain much that otherwise is inexplicable, and, as has been truly said, must be accepted as the "limitation and not the manifestation of the final principle of life."[1]

While, then, to the Vedântist the world in its last

[1] Lidgett's *Fatherhood of God*, p. 373.

explanation is an unreality, to the Christian it is a true manifestation of the character and purpose of God; something, therefore, which must be studied with reverent attention and wondering gratitude.

ii. But S′ankara's idealism not only disparages nature; it equally discredits man. It places him, with all his parts and faculties, in exactly the same class as the surrounding physical phenomena. He, like them, is simply one movement in the everlasting dream of Brahma. His instincts and intuitions, therefore, are fundamentally unreliable, and the testimony of his consciousness ought properly to be repudiated at every turn. The Vedântist thus finds himself in a very singular position; he is compelled every day and all day long to assume something which his theory pronounces false, and then to act on the assumption. He eats and drinks, loves and hates, plans and trusts, and his whole life consists in these things; and yet behind all and through all he has the assurance, born of his hypothesis, that he is the illusory victim of a baseless phantasy. In this way a man is completely torn in two: bound by circumstance to live, he is bound by his doctrine to regard his life as unreal. To the serious-minded man such a chronic internal schism should be a continual distress and despair. But most of the disciples of S′ankara, in these days at any rate, seem disposed to attend to the phenomenal in the confidence that the real will take care of itself. "You have jewels," said I to a Vedântin one day; "if I possess myself of them, will you turn philosopher and reflect that your possession of the jewels and my appropriation of them are alike an illusion, and send no policeman after me?" The Vedântin smiled a slow wise smile, and thus replied—"Your illustration is good, but you do not carry it far enough. I will certainly send the policeman after you and put you in prison; and when you get there, *you* may reflect that that is an illusion also." This represents with fair accuracy the spirit in which the average Indian pantheist treats his great doctrine. But wherever it is received with conviction it can only issue in discouragement. For it reduces knowledge to fiction and takes the heart out of enterprise. Why should men encounter discomfort and danger and loss to add to the sum of human knowledge, or to the comfort and efficiency of human life, when all is illusion? From among men fed on a theory like this you are never likely to get a Bacon or a Newton, a Howard or a Wilberforce, a Franklin or a Livingstone. But knowledge of the Divine is as impossible, on this theory, as knowledge of the secular is untrustworthy. Brahma alone is in the realms of the Real. I myself, and all like me, are unreal entities moving only in the realms of the Unreal. How, then, is the gulf to be bridged? How is the Unreal ever to know the Real? If, as we are told, the faculty that apprehends is false, then must its apprehension be false also. But if perchance the Unreal *could* cross the gulf and enter the domain of the Real, it must itself cease at that instant to exist, and its apprehensions must therefore cease with it! It has been said that, on this theory, "I can only know God by ceasing to be man"; but when I cease to be, I cease to know, and the flash of insight that annihilates the illusory me—what can it be but the false apprehension of a false entity? Be that as it may, the Vedântist agrees that if the light that shines within—my real Self—would stream forth and join the Universal Light (though that Light is one and indivisible), then the pitcher that encloses it—this personality of mine—must first be broken and for ever cast aside. Thus, then, we see that Vedântism disparages man as well as nature by attributing unreality to his best faculties, and by denying that his knowledge has any correspondence with ultimate fact.

iii. It is simply one specific deduction from the above statement when we say that Vedântism entirely discredits the moral sense in man. We talk about conscience, and regard it as the supreme faculty in our constitution; but to the Hindu, conscience, like will and taste and judgment, is merely phenomenal, and the distinctions which it makes between right and wrong have only a temporary and conventional value. "If you tell the truth," says the Vedântist Hindu, "conscience can only be described as a fiction, and morality and duty as part of the obligation imposed by that fiction. In this dream-world the concern is not whether you are doing good actions or bad ones. That is a minor consideration. The concern is that you should act at all—for *all* action brings consequences and prolongs the period that we must spend on the wheel." In presence of this theory, the distinction between virtue and vice becomes as unimportant as (say) the distinction between refinement and coarseness, smartness and stupidity, a sanguine temperament and a phlegmatic one. The only distinction worth making is that between the phenomenal and the real, and the rest is as nothing. Clearly in such a system it is utterly beside the mark to speak about sin. That is as much an illusion as everything else. All deeds are in themselves the same. Speaking phenomenally, there are certain activities which are inconvenient, inasmuch as they bring upon us misfortune or disaster; while other activities are desirable because they bring us comfort and credit. But essentially there is no difference, so that we are free to choose any course of action that expediency seems to suggest. If it will help a man to enjoyment or to promotion to tell a lie, then a lie is as good as the truth; it is only to be regretted when it fails, but for that matter the truth would be equally regrettable if it happened to bring trouble. Sin, therefore, if it be acknowledged to exist at all, is nothing other than *the transgression of expediency;* the failure to secure your pleasure safely, the exposing yourself in any form to avoidable misfortune or inconvenience. And what is holiness? Still speaking phenomenally, holiness is only *the perfection of prudence.* To do nothing that will make you obnoxious to your caste, or to the larger community around you, is a very fair attainment in holiness. What a man may do safely, that he may do confidently. Hence it is that in India there is such a shifting standard of morals. The gods may do, and be lauded for doing, that which in a man would be execrated and punished: the 'peccadilloes' of Krishna, *e.g.*, are celebrated in popular 'sacred' song; and when you challenge them you are informed that he was a god, and had the power and the right to do as he would, but that human beings, not having the same power, may not claim the same indulgence. Similarly, among men, the rajah has one standard of conduct, while the subject must accommodate himself to another; the zemindar may do certain things almost without criticism, which if done by a ryot, would be counted criminal. In India it has been reckoned that might gives moral right—a doctrine which is strongly buttressed by the transmigration theory. For the rest, inward dispositions and secret habits, so far as they do not obtrude themselves upon the outside world to the man's own detriment, are practically unimportant. How completely these ideas have filtered through the various Hindu populations, every one who knows India at all from within is compelled to acknowledge. It is simply a commonplace of careful observation. Every course of conduct, whatever its essential quality, is justified in its success. But in all this we are speaking merely of the phenomenal and from the point of view of the multitude, who illustrate the effects of Vedântism without understanding its philosophy. But when the philosopher himself appears, he brushes aside all phenomenal talk of sin and righteousness and conscience with the impatience of contempt, and leads us back to reality. Seldom, perhaps, has this been stated so artlessly as by the late Swâmi Viv'ekânanda, in one of the addresses which he delivered during the Parliament of Religions in Chicago. "Ye are the children of God," he says, "the sharers of immortal bliss, holy and perfect beings. Ye, divinities on earth, sinners? It is a sin to call a man so. It is a standing libel on human nature. Come up, O lions! and shake off the delusion that you are sheep." The same idea is stated also in a Vedântist publication, the *Brahmavâdin*, in these words:—"The distinctions of right and wrong are mere appearances, which will vanish as soon as the dream state of life is dispelled."[1] We shall have to note shortly

[1] Quoted in Slater's *Higher Hinduism*.

the influence of Vedântism on morality from a slightly different angle, but in the meantime we see that it makes of conscience an illusory faculty, and, except for "practical" purposes, invalidates all its judgments in regard to sin and righteousness. To such a doctrine Christianity stands irreconcilably opposed, affirming, as it does, the trustworthiness and authority of conscience, and the reality and eternity of moral distinctions.

SECTION V

SOME FRUITS OF INDIAN PANTHEISM

THE reader will by this time have realised that the supreme and only tenet of Vedântism is the sole existence of Brahma. The personal God, Îs'vara, is not—except as the illusory product of Mâyâ.[1] Nature and Man in all their

[1] An attempt is sometimes made by Vedântists who have had the advantage of Western education, to deny all essential difference between Brahma and Îs'vara. Thus Mr. K. Sundararâma Iyer, M.A., a very distinguished graduate of the Madras University, in a most interesting article on "God and Jesus in the light of the Vedânta," contributed to the *Madras Review* in November 1901, writes—

"Îs'vara is Brahma *viewed* as related to the Divine Energy and as producing and sustaining the universe, while Brahma is Îs'vara in his essential aspect, as the changeless and noumenal reality. Between Brahma and Îs'vara there is thus a difference in the point of view, and none in essence. They are one and the same being considered in two different aspects, the one expressing the essence of the divine existence, the other emphasising the relation of creator, preserver, and destroyer, in which the one divine entity stands to the universe. Îs'vara is the all-knowing, all-powerful, highest lord of the universe, abides in his own glory, and is all-pervading; but he may take up a special abode, or assume a bodily shape composed of Mâyâ, in order to gratify his devout worshippers, or for the purpose of proclaiming and maintaining virtue, justice, and truth in the world." This is not the true Vedântist view, but merely a modern accommodation of it. Brahma is sole, and has not "two different aspects" until Mâyâ has produced them. There is no Îs'vara at all except as the product of Brahma *plus* Mâyâ. He does not "take up" Mâyâ as a special abode. He does not exist without Mâyâ. His relation to Brahma is unique. He is the original illusion of the impersonal One. The rest of us and the whole material and sentient world are products of that illusion, illusory creatures of an illusory Creator.

qualities and capabilities and activities are the illusory creation of the illusory Îs'vara. But nothing and nobody —whether material world or personal man or personal God —is, except in Brahma. That is the standpoint of the Vedântist philosopher. In the strength of that creed he contradicts the universal testimony of our human consciousness. Joy and sorrow, health and sickness, good and evil, mind and matter, are only name and form superimposed upon the unconscious and unsuspecting Brahma by the irrepressible mischief-maker Mâyâ. But a standpoint like this is too subtle to be adopted by the popular mind, and when the Vedântist has cried—"Nothing is but in God," the common man has translated the high saying into another—"God is in everything"! It was inevitable, and the philosophers themselves have acquiesced in it. God is in everything—a being undistinguishingly diffused throughout His creation, as closely related, therefore, to any one thing, the lowest, as to any other thing, the highest, independently of all moral considerations. A Vedântist cannot shrink from allowing, for instance, that God is as truly present in brute matter as in sentient life; that He is as certainly manifested in carnal appetite as in intellectual achievement; that He is as closely present to the selfish heart as He is to the generous hand.

> To him who wisely sees,
> The Brahman with his scrolls and sanctities,
> The cow, the elephant, the unclean dog,
> The Outcast gorging dog's meat, all are one.

So sings the *Bhagavad Gîta*, and the sentiment has

found its way into the folk-songs of Southern India. Thus we read—

> Where God is seen there can be nought but God.
> His heart can have no place for fear or shame;
> For caste, uncleanness, hate, or wandering thought,
> Impure or pure, are all alike to Him.[1]

Frequently in conversation there is thrown around these ideas the interest of illustration and the glamour of poetry. The sunshine, they will say, streams upon all things with imperial indiscrimination. It burnishes the hilltop, but it does not disdain the dunghill; it flashes in the clear mountain stream, but it lends its glory also to the stagnant pool. Whatever the thing in itself, the presence of the sunlight consecrates it, and he who would do reverence to the sunlight may do it just as legitimately and just as effectually in presence of the stagnant pool as of the running brook. The application is plain. Is not God, like the sunlight, everywhere: in me, in the stone, the snake, the cow? All things are worshipful because God is in them all, and the only consideration that need regulate one's worship is that of custom or convenience. Thus idolatry is everywhere in India, and finds its reason and justification in the Pantheism that pervades India. Every mountain-top is the pedestal of some deity; every roadside has numerous shapes inviting men to worship. The philosophic creed of India has suffered, at the hands of the people, the most degrading translation. Images no bigger than an infant's toy, and forms "more foul than bacchanals, more monstrous than the fancies of nightmare," are worshipped with low prostration. Surely never was more

[1] Translated by Gover.

fearful Nemesis. Indian Pantheism began by sublimating everything into God; it has continued by precipitating God into everything. The subtlest spiritual monism in the world lives in open and unashamed alliance with the grossest idolatry.

But it does not conclude there. If the Vedântist cannot deny that God is present in every form of phenomenal existence, he must allow also that He is present in every form of activity, and this again independently of all moral considerations. He must, for instance, confess that God is as truly present in lustful scheming and cruel act as in the most splendid self-renunciation and the most magnanimous courtesy. "One to ME are shame and fame." What, then, is right and what wrong, when all is the outcome of the same energy? God is as the wind, man is as the sea. The sea writhes in wrath or smiles in peace, just as the wind will. It carries rich freights in safety to distant ports, or dashes the ships against the rocks, just as the wind will. The wind is inexorable, the sea is irresponsible. That is the true parable of Pantheism. Who are we to question the energy of God? We cannot control it; still less may we evade it. We are the vehicles of its manifestation, that is all. Everywhere and in all things man is the driven victim of God. A creed like that does two things: it relieves men of all true sense of responsibility; it also paralyses hope and permanently bars progress. It converts men into the phonographs of God—incapable and irresponsible by themselves; simply registering and repeating the utterances of another. This is, in truth, the effect of this doctrine upon the people. Far more than can be imagined by strangers to India, men are blaming back upon God their meannesses and impurities, their sorrows and crimes, and gaining thereby the peace of irresponsibility. At an up-country station jail once I saw a man standing with hands pinioned, in charge of a small band of sepoys, and was told that he was just being taken to be hanged. When I expressed my regret at the trouble which his crime had brought upon him, the man's eyes flashed, and he said—"*I* didn't kill the man; it was God that did it. Don't you know that all we do is God's doing?" That was no mere excuse. I have no doubt the man sincerely believed himself to be the irresponsible agent of a Power that he could neither resist nor escape. The incident affords an extreme, and perhaps somewhat dramatic, illustration of a sentiment which is very widely diffused. Among certain classes in India there is no more pressing need than that the people should have their personality disentangled for them, and should be set forth to themselves as separate, free, and therefore responsible. We need to tell them that, when one man kills another, it is not God in that man who has been committing murder. We need to tell the women of India, labouring under cruel disabilities, that they need no longer acquiesce in them, under the idea that it is God who compels them to marry as infants and degrades them when they become widows. It will be a good day for India when men have reached the conviction that custom is not infallibly the incarnation of God, for that He is holy and only holy, just and wholly just, and good without any admixture of evil; eternally separate from the inhumanities of custom, from the impurities of mythology, and from the cruel partialities of caste.

We have seen how Vedântism affects the Hindu in regard to worship and morality. Let us ask how it stands in relation to the great question of human brotherhood. One would presume that here, at least, its record would be good. For Vedântism is at bottom the doctrine of the One Real. That, therefore, which has any claim to reality in any of us is exactly the same in all. Speaking as a Vedântist and in terms of ultimate truth, *I am my brother*, whatever his race, colour, or language, and I am bound by my hypothesis to try to penetrate to and identify the One Soul in each separate illusory incarnation of it. Or if I leave the real and turn to the empirical, I am still committed by this doctrine to the recognition of a common relationship among men; for in another than the apostolic sense, "there is no difference": we are all victims of the same illusion, and needing, and struggling towards, the same deliverance. Theoretically, therefore, caste, which divides men by impassable chasms, should find no countenance in Vedântism. Actually, however, it has found therein constant support and justification. Why should this have been? It is due in part, no doubt, to the fact that a system of thought which traces all that is to God, and thereby makes revolt and reform an impiety, was not likely to oppose a social arrangement which it found already in existence and well established. But it is also certainly due to the other fact, that that social arrangement brought enormous advantage to its own chief adherents. S'ankara, for one, never wearies of affirming the sacred obligation of caste distinctions for everybody, except the man who has attained final knowledge; and such an one, he tells us, though free, is of all men least likely to violate established tradition.

Vedântism has rendered an important service to the caste system by providing for it a sort of philosophic basis. Its primary postulate, as we know, is that Brahma is sole, and that all else is illusion. That illusion is universal, however, and so long as it lasts we must accommodate ourselves to it. What, then, can be better *than that the illusory life should be lived as nearly as possible on the analogy of the real?* In the realm of the real Brahma is the supreme entity; in the realm of illusion *the community* counts as the corresponding entity. Religiously, the source of all evil and misery is the retention of personal human consciousness; socially, the one unforgiveable sin is the assertion of personal freedom. Just as, the moment we touch reality, the one unconditioned Brahma necessarily annihilates all separate existence, so in this world of phenomena the social whole legitimately crushes out all individual rights and pretensions. That, in truth, is the singular and distinctive work of caste—the depression of the individual and the exaltation of the community; and Vedântism has probably, by its "pseudo-philosophical justification," done more than any other school of thought to rivet upon India an organisation by which the sense of separate responsibility is practically extinguished, and conscience, as the organ of moral freedom, is killed. Society, which *claims* to be sacred, tyrannises completely over personality, which *ought* to be sacred. How complete that tyranny is, is only faintly realised by those who have lived all their life in the West. In spite of much that has been written to the contrary, the social conventions of Europe, even where most rigid, bear only a very superficial analogy to the caste system of India. *They* do not fix a man finally in any one class; there are large areas of life which they do not affect at all; and they are never enforced by religious sanctions. But caste fixes a man's position, determines his obligations, decides his direction quite independently of his individual gifts, character, or predilections. It hedges him in on every side, and that from the very first. A man may not, in disobedience to its regulations, assert the right of individual human love to select its own affinity, and his marriage is therefore arranged for him in childhood without his consent being required. A man may not, except within very narrow limits, assert the right of natural aptitude; and many a young priestly Brâhman, who could certainly have carved out a fortune for himself as a merchant, is living the life of a 'religious' beggar. Caste thwarts educated taste;—which is the reason why such multitudes of educated Hindus, with the desire and the means to visit Europe, are permanently imprisoned within their own shores. Nay, a Hindu may not assert even the right to life, if the condition of living is the breaking of some conventional caste rule. During a great famine in the Mysore, I saw a man lying exhausted on the roadside. "What is the matter?" I asked. "I am very hungry," said the man; "for three days I have tasted no rice." I bade him keep up heart, and leaving him for a time I presently reappeared with a leaf plate, and on the plate a mound of cooked rice, every grain white and separate, as the Hindu loves to have it. "Eat a little," I urged, "and you will feel better." The man looked at the rice most eagerly; and then at me most piteously; but at last, shaking his hand very feebly, he said—"*Bêḍayya bêḍa; nanna jâti, nanna jâti*" ("I daren't, I daren't; my caste, my caste"). "But if you don't eat, you cannot live," I gently persisted. To this he only replied—"*Jâti hôdare, prâṇavênu*" ("If I lose my caste, what is the good of my life?"). I was in a remote part of the country, and unable to call any one to his assistance. Caste rules forbade his taking cooked food from the hand of a stranger and foreigner, and in his loyalty to them he declined the only help available. He died before the day was done. The truth is, as I think Dr. Miller has somewhere said, "Hinduism has so effectually overborne and crushed out the individual elements in life, so strengthened and exalted the social, that the Hindu lives and moves and has his being not in himself at all, but in the community of which he forms so insignificant a part. Its thoughts are his, its feelings his. Whatever impulse seizes it, passes unresisted over him. With the community he is willing to do anything, move anywhere in belief or thought; without it he will not move, nor will he usually acknowledge any obligation to move." Times are changing even in India, and the temper of the Hindu is changing with the times. But the words which I have quoted are an accurate description of the real spirit and working of the caste system, and they are substantially true to-day. For the continuance of that system, Vedântism has a large share of responsibility. Not only has it never repudiated it, it has frankly adopted it and strenuously fought in its defence. This fact is not very palatable to present-day Vedântists who have come into touch with the larger and nobler influences of their time, and who delight to show what strong support the sentiment of universal brotherhood *might* find in their system. But they cannot deny history, and S'ankara is completely against them.

SECTION VI

VEDÂNTISM AS A RELIGION

As the hart panteth after the water brooks, so panteth my soul after Thee, O God.—PSALM xlii. 1.

If ye then, being evil, know how to give good gifts unto your children; how much more shall your heavenly Father give the Holy Spirit to them that ask Him?—ST. LUKE ix. 13.

WE have exhibited Indian Pantheism in its theoretical implications and in some of its practical developments. It remains for us to consider whether it has any value as a religion.

I

The necessary notes of religion are adoration, trust, and love, and it finds its natural exercise in prayer and thanksgiving. But these feelings and exercises are impossible unless we first of all postulate a distinction of persons between God and the worshipper. "God is God, and I am I; He one person, and I another." Without that religion has no meaning. Now Vedântism affirms with the strongest emphasis God's presence in us; but it denies with equal emphasis that He is personally distinct from us. Dr. Deussen quite truly states the Vedântic position thus:—"(1) The soul cannot be different from Brahma, because besides Brahma there is no being; (2) it cannot be regarded as a transformation of Brahma, because Brahma is unchangeable; (3) and still less is it a part of Brahma, because Brahma has no parts. Nothing remains, then, but to conclude that the soul is identical with Brahma—that each one of us is the all-unchangeable Brahma, without parts, and comprehending in itself all being." This is a severely careful statement, and needs no confirmation. But it may be well to set by the side of it the witness of one of India's own sons, the late Swâmi Vivékânanda. In one of his lectures he asks—"Why does man go out to look for a God? . . . It is your own heart beating, and you did not know; you were mistaking it for something external. He, nearest of the near, my own self, the reality of my own life, my body and my soul,—I am Thee and Thou art Me. That is your own nature. Assert it, manifest it. . . . You are not to be perfect, you are that already."[1] These are not ecstatic ejaculations struck out suddenly in a moment of oratorical excitement. They are the first and final word of the Vedânta.[2] But if they were true they would render worship an enormity. A theory like this transforms every act of reverent adoration into an act of mere self-glorification. The moment when a man worships ought to be the moment when he most nearly touches reality, and if at such a time a man shall say to himself—"In sober truth I am Brahma, enmeshed, indeed, for the time being

[1] See several passages of this sort quoted in James' *Varieties of Religious Experience*, pp. 513, 514.

[2] Compare the *Chhândogya Upanishad*, III. 14:—"The universal soul is my soul within the heart; smaller than a grain of rice, a barley corn, a mustard-seed, a grain of millet, or the kernel of a grain of millet. This is my soul within the heart, greater than the earth, the air, the sky, greater than these worlds."

in Mâyâ and hoodwinked by many a delusion, but Brahma nevertheless, and there is no other"—all possibility of worship is past. At times when earthly distress forces the man into an attitude of prayer, is it not inevitable that a sudden doubt should arrest his petition, and that he should cry—"Alas! I am speaking only to myself"?

When we leave this high ground, and consider man merely in his phenomenal character, we are still as far as ever from finding a religion in Vedântism. For the God that it presents to us is impersonal, having neither parts nor passion; neither eyes to see, nor ears to hear, nor a heart to feel. Why praise the deaf? Why prostrate yourself before the blind? Why wail to the unfeeling? Why order your arguments before the unknowing? If God be such, every temple for worship, every sacrifice in propitiation, every act of prayer, and every psalm of thanksgiving is a superfluity and the very wantonness of unreason. Little wonder that *The Hindu*, an influential newspaper in Madras, has written—"The Vedântic God is a cold, dreary, philosophic conception, which the Hindu masses have never cared for, which the vast majority of mankind can never be brought to reverence, and which is quite incapable of influencing them in the formation of character."[1]

Strangely enough, and yet perhaps not strangely, we find our Indian philosophers commending to their followers *Bhakti* (*i.e.* loving devotion) as one path leading to final illumination and deliverance. It is not regarded as the highest path, but it is counted as a good and sure way, if withal a slow one, by which to reach the Vedântic heaven.

[1] Quoted in Slater's *Higher Hinduism*, p. 123.

Loving devotion! But love can only be when there is an object that excites it, and it is only satisfied when that object responds to it. Mere spontaneous love, which has no relation to a real and worthy object, is simply the phantasy of an ill-regulated brain; and love which can gain no response either dies unfed or turns life into a lasting bitterness. How then can one love Brahma? According to the hypothesis, he has no qualities to evoke love and no faculty with which to recognise and respond to it.

> . . . Brahma is bodiless and actionless,
> Passionless, calm, unqualified.

In regard to such an entity love is as impossible as hate.

Love in its truest sense is always of persons to persons, and it is in recognition of this fact that the Vedânta finds room within itself for the doctrine of a personal God. A Western Pantheist has said—"The universal does not attract us until housed in an individual." By evolving Îs′vara the Hindu has sought to bring the universal into bounds, and to set forth the uninteresting abstract in the form of an attractive concrete. If, however, this Îs′vara were real he would still be no true manifestation of Brahma. For he is personal, endowed with intelligence and purpose and love, and therefore no contemplation of him, no approach in spirit unto him, could ever help us one step towards knowing *it*. But he is *not* real. He is the first and chief of all illusions, the earliest offspring of Brahma's union with Mâyâ. He stands, therefore, in the same category of phenomena as ourselves, and needs the same enlightenment as we do to dispel his illusion. With this knowledge present to his mind, how is it possible for any man, when his thought is clearest and his purpose most sincere, to turn to Îs′vara with reverence and desire and self-committal, all of which are essential to true religious love? Who can become enthusiastically devoted to an admitted fiction? To bid us worship a personal God, and to tell us at the same time that such a God is, in truth, only a phantasm, is to mock and degrade us—if indeed it be possible to degrade unreal beings such as we are.

Vedântism, then, offers to man no real object of religious affection; neither does it present to him any Being to whom he can pray. The instinct of prayer is universal. Men are always needing, always asking, and always supposing themselves to be near a Presence that can answer them. By the witness of multitudes through long ages there is no exercise which so certainly comforts, strengthens, and purifies the soul as prayer. But the Vedântist cannot consistently suggest either use or suitability in that exercise. He might almost as well be an atheist and deny the existence of God altogether as postulate such a real entity as Brahma, or such a phenomenal person as Îs′vara. Addressed to such beings prayer simply loses itself in the air, and cannot strike echoes anywhere. It is a relief to turn from unintelligent irresponsive Impersonality, and from a merely mythical Personality, to Him of Whom our Lord said—"When ye pray, say, FATHER."[1] Father! In that word we have, with real personality, kinship, authority, and love. All the elements that suggest reverence, evoke affection, and promise satisfaction, are united in the Father. To a God who is Father sons properly

[1] St. Luke xi. 2 (R.V.).

render devotion and address petition, and thus all that makes religion becomes possible.

II

Vedântism fails as a religion because it presents an impossible object of devotion; but it fails also because it misdirects the appeal which it makes in man. To the Vedântist the trouble at the root of all things is not sin—a disordered and unsubmissive will; but ignorance—a darkened understanding. The remedy, therefore, which he announces is not moral but metaphysical. That is the distinctive mark of that great system: it makes its appeal almost solely to the intellect, and relegates such other faculties of man as will and affection, to inferior esteem and attention. S′ankara, in the very forefront of his commentary on the *Vedânta-Sûtras*, places these words:—"With a view to freeing one's self from that wrong notion which is the cause of all evil, and ascertaining thereby the knowledge of the absolute unity of the Self, the study of the Vedânta texts is begun."[1] "Wrong notion"—that is the evil; "knowledge"—that is the cure. Here is set forth the complete Vedântic diagnosis of man's state and its main scheme for obtaining salvation. According to this, the Hindu need not concern himself anxiously about an obedient will or purged affections; he need not cry with the Psalmist, "Create in me a clean heart, O God, and renew a right spirit within me." If he does this there can be no objection, but he is thereby concentrating his attention on subordinate faculties and an inferior aim.

[1] *Vedânta-Sûtras* (*S.B.E.*), p. 9.

Now, such a grading of our faculties has no authority in experience and is impossible to religion. Kant had strong justification when he dismissed Pure Reason from sovereignty in regard to religion, and affirmed instead the "primacy of the Practical Reason"—"the validity and transcendent authority of those notions which are involved in our moral personality."[1] The will is *par excellence* the moral faculty. The cognitive faculty is non-moral. There may be knowledge of God and yet estrangement from Him. There is no ground for the assumption that progressive knowledge will certainly mean approximating union, or for the hope that perfect knowledge will inevitably end in complete identity. Religion is fundamentally the reconciliation of persons and not the solving of metaphysical problems. The clearest apprehension of God's nature may yet leave us far from submission and love—in which case, however advanced we may be in philosophy, religion has not yet begun.

The distinction between Christianity and Vedântism on this point has been so clearly set forth by Dr. Deussen in his great work on the "Philosophy of the Upanishads," that we must needs, though dissenting in part, quote nearly the whole of it. He says—"Why do we need a release from this existence? Because it is the realm of sin, is the reply of the Bible. The Veda answers, Because it is the realm of ignorance. The former sees depravity in the volitional, the latter in the intellectual side of man. The Bible demands a change of the will, the Veda of the understanding. On which side does the truth lie? If man were pure will or pure intelligence, we should have

[1] See *Teaching of Swâmi Vivêkânanda*, p. 68.

to decide for one or the other alternative. But since he is a being who both wills and knows, the great change upon which the Bible and the Veda alike make salvation depend must be fully wrought out in both departments of the life. Such a change is, in the first place, according to the biblical view, the softening of a heart hardened by natural self-love, and the inclining of it to deeds of righteousness, affection, and self-denial. But it is, in the second place, the breaking forth upon us of the light of the great intellectual truth, which the Upanishads taught before Kant, that this entire universe with its relations to space, its consequent manifoldness and dependence upon the mind that apprehends, rests solely upon an illusion (*mâyâ*), natural indeed to us through the limitations of our intellect; and that there is in truth one Being alone, eternal, exalted above space and time, multiplicity and change, revealed in all the forms of nature, and by me who also am one and undivided, discovered, and realised within as my very Self, the Âtman. As surely, however, as to adopt the significant teaching of Schopenhauer, the will and not the intellect is the centre of a man's nature, so surely must the pre-eminence be assigned to Christianity in that its demand for a renewal of the will is peculiarly vital and essential. But, on the other hand, as certainly as man is not mere will, but intellect besides, so certainly will that Christian renewal reveal itself on the other side as a renewal of knowledge, just as the Upanishads teach."[1]

In this passage Dr. Deussen's suggested parallel

[1] Translated by Professor Geden in an article in the *London Quarterly Review*.

between Bible and Vedântic teaching is vitiated by this one consideration, that the Bible postulates a real man with a responsible will, while the Veda postulates an illusory man with an unreal intellect, and capable only of a false apprehension. But, setting that aside, we may remark that in Christianity the insistence on the primacy of the moral faculties in man does not, in the slightest degree, involve the disparagement of the intellectual faculties. Illumination is as much an object of desire to the Christian as to the Hindu, but he finds the surest path to it in obedience, which is of the will. "If any man willeth to do His will he shall know of the doctrine."[1] The knowledge which springs from spiritual sympathy and loyal devotion is not less clear and full than that which comes from mere intellectual apprehension. And it has this great advantage, that it may be acquired by all. Speculative aptitudes are the possession only of the few. But moral aptitudes are given to all; in differing degrees no doubt, and with differing completeness of result, but still to all. It is on this side, therefore, that Christianity makes its principal appeal. To win your way to the final bliss of the Vedânta you must be a philosopher; for though the beatific vision transcends reason, yet metaphysical knowledge is the necessary preparation for it. But Christianity presents not the problems of the Divine being, but the perfections of the Divine character. It exhibits to us His grace, His patience, His forgiving mercy, His constant care—traits which make successful appeal to the apprehension of all —and bids us respond with a ready will and grateful

[1] St. John vii. 17 (R.V.).

heart, with humility, submission, and trust. It would lead us to God by the pathway of moral accord with Him, not intellectual comprehension of Him. Vedântism is a system framed for the few who delight in subtleties and revel in debate; but, while it quickens mental perception, it neither warms the affections nor rectifies the will. Christianity, on the other hand, seeks to produce moral renovation, and thereby takes the first step towards inspiring, directing, illuminating, and saving the whole man.

III

Whither does this system lead? If we accept its premises and follow its precepts, to what goal shall we attain? The answer lies in the one word MUKTI, *i.e.* Liberation. That is India's great word. It represents the *summum bonum*, the final bliss. It is not heaven; it is a state greater and better than that. Heaven (*svarga*) is but one stage to *mukti*, a coveted and delectable experience indeed, but transient even as hell (*naraka*) is transient.

> . . . they, when that prodigious joy is o'er,
> Paradise spent, and wage for merits given,
> Come to the world of death and change once more.

But in *mukti* the last birth has been reached, the chain of works that bound us to phenomena is broken, and the transmigrating entity has won home at last. This result is attained through *vidyâ, i.e.* knowledge. The life-long effort of the pilgrim is to know himself as he really is—in himself and apart from phenomena. "*Γνῶθι σεαυτόν* meant a very different thing to the Greek and to the devout disciple of Upanishad teaching. To the latter γνῶσις was an opening of the eyes, the recognition of an existing fact which only needed to be known and realised to bring about, automatically as it were, his release from the pains and penalties of existence, and the enjoyment of tranquil and ceaseless repose. There was therefore no question of an absorption or reabsorption into Brahma. Such a phrase was meaningless, and the conception involved irrational and self-contradictory. *He already was, and always had been, one with Brahma.* Blinded, however, by Mâyâ, he had lost sight of this fundamental, this all-important truth, and had wandered far in the mazes of error and deceit. With the recovery of knowledge there had come also to the newly-enlightened man recovery of bliss."[1]

"One with Brahma"—that is the goal, *mukti.* But what, precisely, does that represent? We must here put away all our Western notions of matured powers working with the zest and harmony of perfect health in an eternally congenial environment. It is the exact truth to say that *mukti* is not "perfect character, but perfect characterlessness." One with Brahma? But in Brahma there is neither thought, nor will, nor feeling. It is Being, in a dreamless sleep that shall never be broken. It has no interests, no activities, no positive enjoyments. Its happiness is the blank monotony of eternal, unintelligent repose. The nearer, then, the pilgrim, while still pursuing his journey, can approximate to this condition, the sooner may he hope to reach his goal. The man closest to Brahma is he whose phenomenal interests have been most successfully

[1] Professor Geden in *London Quarterly Review.*

narrowed, whose necessary activities are emptiest of care and desire, whose faculties have been most nearly atrophied. That man is farthest away from Brahma who is most wide-awake, whose interests are most vivid, whose activities are most catholic, and whose faculties are at the highest point of responsiveness and efficiency. To the Vedântist, therefore, final salvation means, not the filling of life to the farthest limits of its capacity, but the complete emptying of it. In so far as his thoughts move in line with his system, his ideal must be poles apart from all that we mean by great and true manhood.

The religious discipline approved by the Vedânta accords exactly with the end to be attained. The Self is believed to be encased in five vestures—(1) the earthly body, (2) the vital airs, (3) the sensorial, (4) the cognitional, and (5) the beatific vestures. The second, third, and fourth of these form the invisible body, which accompanies the soul through all its pilgrimage of births. But it is only when the last and innermost of these vestures has been stripped away that the Self is free and *mukti* is realised. How, then, is this five-fold encasement to be laid aside? In the main, and most successfully, by the practice of those forms of asceticism prescribed by the Yóga discipline.[1] Yóga means "union," and the elaborate and difficult directions given to the practising Yógî are all meant to speed the union of the individual spirit with the sole and eternal Self, by withdrawing it progressively from everything phenomenal. The discipline first of all prescribes acts of "forbearance"

[1] "If a man practises Yóga for six months and is thoroughly free from the outer world, then the perfect union, which is endless, high, and hidden, is accomplished."—*Maitrâyaṇa-Upanishad*, IV. 28.

(*yama*)—forbearing to slay, to indulge the passions, to receive gifts. But this is very elementary, and the real meaning and method of Yóga only become apparent when we reach the section dealing with religious postures (*âsana*).[1]

In a fair, still spot
Having fixed his abode,—not too much raised,
Nor yet too low,—let him abide, his goods
A cloth, a deerskin, and the Kuśa grass.
There, setting hard his mind upon The One,
Restraining heart and senses, silent, calm,
Let him accomplish Yóga, and achieve
Pureness of soul, *holding immovable*
Body and neck and head, his gaze absorbed
Upon his nose end, rapt from all around.[2]

In this typical posture the Yógî is to practise three methods of restraining and ultimately of suspending the breathing (*prâṇâyâma*); he is to persist in the practice of them until he becomes oblivious of everything around him, and is able to meditate without recognising distinction of subject and object! When he can repeat the mystic syllable *Om* in silence 20,736,000 times and meditate uninterruptedly upon it, and when he can suspend the respiratory movements completely for a period of twelve days, then the Yógî has arrived at *samâdhi*—the state in which *mukti* is close at hand.[3] But *samâdhi* is a state of trance, of self-hypnotism, of the complete arrest of all outward correspondences. One to him who has reached

[1] The eight accessories of Yóga are :—(1) Forbearance (*yama*), (2) Minor religious observances (*niyama*), (3) Religious postures (*âsana*), (4) Regulation of the breath (*prâṇâyâma*), (5) Restraint of the organs of sense (*pratyâhâra*), (6) Fixed attention (*dhâraṇa*), (7) Contemplation (*dhyâna*), (8) Meditation (*samâdhi*).

[2] Sir Edwin Arnold's *Song Celestial*, Chapter vi.

[3] See Jacob's *Hindu Pantheism*, p. 120.

that state are "heat and cold, pleasures and pain, glory and shame." He is

> dwelling apart
> Upon a peak, with senses subjugate,
> Whereto the clod, the rock, the glistering gold
> Show all as one.

The process of salvation is thus, in the Vedânta, one of progressive self-circumscription—the exclusion of interests until the last has disappeared, the persistent repression of thought until thoughtlessness has been reached. The Vedântic saint is the man who has pursued abstraction to the point of vacuity, who has declined from passivity to absolute apathy, who has reached perfect inertion. Henceforth nothing connected with the phenomenal world can delight or depress him.

> . . . like the ocean, day by day receiving
> Floods from all lands, which never overflows;
> Its boundary line not leaping, and not leaving,
> Fed by the rivers, but unswelled by those;—
>
> So is the perfect one! to his soul's ocean
> The world of sense pours streams of witchery;
> They leave him as they find, without commotion,
> Taking their tribute, but remaining sea.

He has eyes, but is as if he walked in darkness; ears, but dwells as in unbroken stillness; a mind, but knows not this from that. He has renounced all—home, friends, interests, ambitions, and even personality itself.[1] Though he lives on, he is

> Unmoved by passions and unbound by deeds,
> Setting result aside.

[1] "If a man, though well enlightened (by instruction), is still pierced by passion and darkness, and attached to his children, wife, and house, then perfect union is never accomplished."—*Maitrâyaṇa-Upanishad*, VI. 28.

Upon the man thus prepared the vision breaks at last. He sees his own self as the Highest Self,[1] and in the brightness of that vision all lesser lights—the "I" and "thou" and "it" of phenomenal life—fade as stars at sunrise. He is able to say—"In pure verity it is only the Self that ever is or has been. There has been no soul migrating, neither any world in which it wept and hoped and toiled. These things were phantasmagoric figments, a play of semblances, an illusory darkness. Now the light is unveiled, and it is a pure undifferenced light. I AM BRAHMA, and there is no other, nothing else."[2] Thus "the dewdrop slips into the shining sea," and *mukti* is attained. With clear apprehension he makes the great final confession of Vedântism—BRAHMA SATYAM, JAGAN MITHYÂ, JÎVA BRAHMAIVA NÂPARA (Brahma is true, the world is false, the soul is Brahma and nothing else).

This is an experience, we are told, which may be obtained in our present life. It is the ambition of every true Vedântist to become a *jîvanmukta*—one, *i.e.*, liberated from further succession of births, and still living. A single illustration is enough to suggest to the Hindu the possibility of this. Just as the potter's wheel may continue to revolve long after the force that started it has been withdrawn, so the phenomenal life may continue even after Ignorance, which caused it, has been dispelled. Now the special mark of the *jîvanmukta*, the man who has scaled the topmost summit of Vedântic sainthood, is this—that he has penetrated the illusion of plurality,

[1] *Maitrâyaṇa-Upanishad*, VI. 20.

[2] Cf. Gough's *Philosophy of the Upanishads*, p. 61, from which some of these phrases are reproduced.

and knows there is nothing but the One. All things, therefore, and all deeds are to him one and the same. Distinctions of every kind are finally obliterated. He knows "the secondless Reality," and is no longer deceived by such mere names as right and wrong, fair and foul! "To him a thief is not a thief, a murderer not a murderer, an outcast not an outcast."[1] Thenceforward he is free to do what he will, without fear and without rebuke, for he knows that there is nothing but Brahma, and that *he* is Brahma. "If he sees the unity of all things, he is unaffected, alike whether he offer a hundred horse-sacrifices or kill hundreds of holy Brâhmans."[2] Ânandagiri, the disciple and exponent of S'ankara, says—"The perfect sage, so long as he lives, may do good and evil as he chooses, and incur no stain; such is the efficacy of a knowledge of the Self." Other men are bound by caste rules, but to this emancipated one there are none. He may cross the seas, mingle indiscriminately with all classes, eat all sorts of food by whomsoever prepared—and all without offence. Other men are bound by a moral code, and if they transgress it, guilt clings to them like "lac to wood." To him all codes are merely conventional, and in the security of his transcendent knowledge he may touch pitch without pollution and drink poison without hurt. "As water does not cling to a lotus leaf, so no evil deed clings to one who knows."[3] Whatever he does, he is supposed to do automatically, without desire or purpose, and therefore without responsibility, and (to himself)

[1] *Bṛihadâraṇyaka-Upanishad*, IV. iii. 22.
[2] Nṛisimhasarasvatî, quoted by Gough.
[3] *Chhândogya-Upanishad*, IV. xiv. 3.

without result. This is the supreme product of Vedântism —a passionless, aimless, unmoral entity, moving in the phenomenal, but presumably engrossed with the real. To such a one, life brings thenceforward neither obligation nor opportunity. There is no further personal development to strive after, and his salvation is perfected in a complete disregard of and indifference to his fellows. He sees them as they are, fugitive shadows, and disesteems them accordingly! Such a being is useful neither for private friendship nor for public service. He is no man. All that makes a man—individuality, energy, interest in great causes, self-sacrificing service for others,—these are absent in him. His feet walk, his hands move, his tongue speaks; but it is merely, as it were, residuary muscular movement, the revolving of the wheel after the impetus that started it has ceased to be applied. Though still *in* the world, he is in no fruitful sense *of* the world. His attainment of liberation has meant his withdrawal from power to help those who are still in the coils of phenomena. So far as they are concerned, he might as well be dead. Principal Gough has said quite truly that it is no business of Indian saints of this type "to seek to see things as they are, and to help to fashion them as they ought to be; to let the power at work in the world work freely through them; to become 'docile echoes of the eternal voice and pliant organs of the infinite will.'"[1] Sainthood in the Vedânta is the dropping of manhood.

The Yóga discipline is the distortion and exaggeration of necessary truth. It is vital for all men that the flesh should be subjugated to spirit, that deed and desire and

[1] *Philosophy of the Upanishads*, p. 267.

thought should be limited for all of us in those directions where they prevent the noblest fruition of our present life or endanger our final destiny. This was the truth enforced by Christ in those great and awful words in which He bids us cut off the hand or foot, or pluck out the eye, if they cause us to stumble.[1] This was what He meant, also, when He bade us renounce home and friends and all that we have, if need be, that we may be His disciples.[2] There is necessity in all lives for self-control, and in most for stern self-curtailment. But it is no base mutilation that our Lord preaches, no process of slow suicide. If there is to be limitation, it is to make us not less of men, but more—stronger and nobler, because we have parted with that which degraded and enfeebled us.

The discipline that He suggests does not ever mean the suppression of life, but its increase and invigoration. His desire for men is not that they should withdraw from the world, but that they should pass through it radiant with energy and overflowing with love, touching it at all points, and touching it always to bless. Jesus is Himself our type as well as our teacher. He was the true Yógî, surrendering Himself absolutely to the will of God, and sacrificing Himself without measure in the service of men. But self-renunciation is not the loss or enfeeblement of manhood; it is its perfect realisation. So was it in the case of our Lord; so is it in every case. "I have been crucified with Christ,"[3] exclaimed Paul. What then? Was the man within him gone? "No," says he, "I live"; and then he explains how

[1] Matt. xviii. 8, 9.
[2] Matt. x. 37; Luke xiv. 33.
[3] Gal. ii. 20 (R.V.)

his life is Christ's life in him, enlarging, permeating and energising his whole being. He yielded up his self completely, and then by God's grace received it back, transmuted, sanctified, completed. Christ calls us all to perfect manhood. When man is at his best, working at most points for the world's highest good, living his life at once most contemplatively and most actively, then is he nearest to union with Him who is the God and Father of us all in Christ Jesus.

CONCLUSION

THE creed of Vedântism may now be summarised. It runs thus:—

> THERE IS ONE—no other, nothing else;
> THOU ART THAT ONE;
> Realise this by whatever rigour of discipline,
> Then misery is past, births are ended, THOU ART SAVED.

To men holding this creed, and shaping their lives and hopes thereby, the Christian Church sends the gospel, the "simple" gospel. If the proclamation of it does not issue in such swift and dramatic success as has been seen in other lands, there need be neither surprise nor despair. For, think what the gospel is. It is the announcement of a personal God; it is the affirmation of the truth of human consciousness; it is the revelation of a God who is holy; it is the assertion of human responsibility and the declaration of the possibility of forgiveness. The "simple" gospel includes all those elements. Anything less than this would be an attenuated gospel, and would have no true relation to the Pantheists of India. Yet on all these points it contradicts the essential teaching of the Vedânta. The disciples of S'ankara, as they listen to it, find themselves in presence, not of subtle harmonies but of staring contrasts. Is it surprising that they doubt and hesitate and turn back? But Christianity will win—not swiftly but surely; for it has on its side common-sense, conscience, and the need of the human heart. In spite of all philosophy, men, and Hindus among them, will be compelled to trust the testimony of their consciousness. In spite of all philosophy, what conscience affirms reason will in vain deny. In spite of all philosophy, the heart will "cry out for God, the living God." The constitution of human nature everywhere is on the side of the gospel of Jesus Christ.

INDEX